THE INTERNET FOR MACS

FOR

DUMMIES™

Quick Reference

by Charles Seiter

IDG
BOOKS

IDG Books Worldwide, Inc.
An International Data Group Company

Foster City, CA ♦ Chicago, IL ♦ Indianapolis, IN ♦ Braintree, MA ♦ Dallas, TX

The Internet For Macs For Dummies Quick Reference

Published by
IDG Books Worldwide, Inc.
An International Data Group Company
919 E. Hillsdale Blvd.
Suite 400
Foster City, CA 94404

Library of Congress Catalog Card No.: 94-79839

ISBN: 1-56884-967-2

Printed in the United States of America

10 9 8 7 6 5 4 3 2 1

1D/QX/RS/ZU

Distributed in the United States by IDG Books Worldwide, Inc.

Distributed by Macmillan Canada for Canada; by Computer and Technical Books for the Caribbean Basin; by Contemporanea de Ediciones for Venezuela; by Distribuidora Cuspide for Argentina; by CITEC for Brazil; by Ediciones ZETA S.C.R. Ltda. for Peru; by Editorial Limusa SA for Mexico; by Transworld Publishers Limited in the United Kingdom and Europe; by Al-Maiman Publishers & Distributors for Saudi Arabia; by Simron Pty. Ltd. for South Africa; by IDG Communications (HK) Ltd. for Hong Kong; by Toppan Company Ltd. for Japan; by Addison Wesley Publishing Company for Korea; by Longman Singapore Publishers Ltd. for Singapore, Malaysia, Thailand and Indonesia; by Unalis Corporation for Taiwan; by WS Computer Publishing Company, Inc. for the Philippines; by WoodsLane Pty. Ltd. for Australia; by WoodsLane Enterprises Ltd. for New Zealand.

For general information on IDG Books in the U.S., including information on discounts and premiums, contact IDG Books 800-434-3422 or 415-655-3000.

For information on where to purchase IDG Books outside the U.S., contact IDG Books International at 415-655-3021 or fax 415-655-3295.

For information on translations, contact Marc Jeffrey Mikulich, Director, Foreign & Subsidiary Rights, at IDG Books Worldwide; 415-655-3018 or fax 415-655-3295.

For sales inquiries and special prices for bulk quantities, write to the address above or call IDG Books Worldwide at 415-655-3000.

For information on using IDG Books in the classroom, or for ordering examination copies, contact Jim Kelly at 800-434-2086.

 is a trademark of IDG Books Worldwide, Inc.

Acknowledgments

I would like to thank Kristin Cocks, my project editor at IDG's Indianapolis office. I would also like to thank those members of the editorial and production staff who gave of their time and talents to make this book a success: Pam Mourouzis, Diane Giangrossi, Jeff Wagonner, Stacey Holden Prince, Cindy Phipps, Chris Collins, Tony Augsburger, and Linda Boyer.

Thanks also to Joanna Pearlstein for tech editing this book.

(The publisher would like to thank Patrick J. McGovern, without whom this book would not have been possible.)

Welcome to the world of IDG Books Worldwide.

IDG Books Worldwide, Inc. is a subsidiary of International Data Group, the world's largest publisher of computer-related information and the leading global provider of information services on information technology. IDG was founded more than 25 years ago and now employs more than 7,000 people worldwide. IDG publishes more than 220 computer publications in 65 countries (see listing below). More than fifty million people read one or more IDG publications each month.

Launched in 1990, IDG Books Worldwide is today the #1 publisher of best-selling computer books in the United States. We are proud to have received 3 awards from the Computer Press Association in recognition of editorial excellence, and our best-selling ...For Dummies™ series has more than 12 million copies in print with translations in 25 languages. IDG Books, through a recent joint venture with IDG's Hi-Tech Beijing, became the first U.S. publisher to publish a computer book in the People's Republic of China. In record time, IDG Books has become the first choice for millions of readers around the world who want to learn how to better manage their businesses.

Our mission is simple: Every IDG book is designed to bring extra value and skill-building instructions to the reader. Our books are written by experts who understand and care about our readers. The knowledge base of our editorial staff comes from years of experience in publishing, education, and journalism — experience which we use to produce books for the '90s. In short, we care about books, so we attract the best people. We devote special attention to details such as audience, interior design, use of icons, and illustrations. And because we use an efficient process of authoring, editing, and desktop publishing our books electronically, we can spend more time ensuring superior content and spend less time on the technicalities of making books.

You can count on our commitment to deliver high-quality books at competitive prices on topics consumers want to read about. At IDG, we value quality, and we have been delivering quality for more than 25 years. You'll find no better book on a subject than an IDG book.

John J. Kilcullen

John Kilcullen
President and CEO
IDG Books Worldwide, Inc.

About the Author

Charles Seiter wrote his first computer programs on ancient IBM iron in the 1960s and, at one point, had a college summer job writing FORTRAN code for Atlas missile guidance simulation. That's right, he *is* a rocket scientist.

Well, not really. He got a Ph.D. in chemistry from Caltech and then worked as a chemistry professor for years. His academic career was derailed by winning a pile of money on a television game show, at which point he freed himself from the job of flunking a certain percentage of premed students in freshman chemistry every year and moved away to a redwood forest in northern California.

He began consulting on the design of DNA sequencing equipment and other biochemistry hardware for firms in the Bay Area and, by chance, just happened to be hanging around when Macworld was founded. Over the course of ten years, he has probably reviewed more Mac technical software than anyone in history. *The Internet For Macs For Dummies Quick Reference* is his 12th computer book and his first in the *...For Dummies Quick Reference* series.

Credits

Executive Vice President, Strategic Product Planning and Research
David Solomon

Editorial Director
Diane Graves Steele

Acquisitions Editor
Megg Bonar

Brand Manager
Judith A. Taylor

Editorial Managers
Tracy L. Barr
Sandra Blackthorn

Editorial Assistants
Tamara S. Castleman
Stacey Holden Prince
Kevin Spencer

Acquisitions Assistant
Suki Gear

Production Director
Beth Jenkins

Production Coordinator
Cindy L. Phipps

Pre-Press Coordinator
Steve Peake

Associate Pre-Press Coordinator
Tony Augsburger

Project Editor
Kristin A. Cocks

Editors
Pamela Mourouzis
Diane Giangrossi
Jeff Wagonner

Technical Reviewer
Joanna Pearlstein

Production Staff
Paul Belcastro
Valery Bourke
Linda Boyer
Chris Collins
Carla Radzikinas
Tricia Reynolds
Gina Scott

Cover Design
Kavish + Kavish

Proofreader
Charles A. Hutchinson

Indexer
David Heiret

Contents at a Glance

Introduction

Greetings! Welcome to *The Internet For Macs For Dummies Quick Reference,* just about the only thing regarding the Internet that's small.

If you use Internet services intermittently, you should keep a copy of this book lying on top of your monitor. That way, you can look up specific step-by-step information when you need it. And you can browse through other chapters while you're waiting for a 2MB file to download!

This is not meant to be a complete guide to all Internet features. As you see in this book and in its companion, *The Internet For Macs For Dummies Starter Kit,* the Internet uses a strange mix of older procedures and easier-to-use newer tools. I could tell you all sorts of Unix tricks, for example, but in a year, you would have no way to practice them. So I'm concentrating on a set of the most useful features for 1995 and beyond.

You will find references throughout the book to different bits of Internet software. It happens that most of the software is free because the Internet started as non-profit. (It's still non-profit, despite all the business activity of the last year or so.) Most of this software is available from any national on-line service, so if you're strolling through a supermarket and see a computer magazine with a free disk attached for America Online or Prodigy, you should know that you can use that disk and free time to collect every piece of Internet shareware you'll need.

And if you have a copy of *The Internet For Macs For Dummies Starter Kit,* you're in even better shape because IDG has collected the most useful Internet software for you already. Then you can just pick a topic here and start working right away.

How to Use This Book

You may note that the parts are arranged as a listing of Internet tools. If you want to find files and retrieve them, just turn to Part IV on Archie and FTP. One part doesn't really "follow" another — you could get a Mosaic connection and never even bother to learn about older Internet programs.

This independence of sections is continued even inside the parts themselves. If you have a particular topic in mind, just look it up in the index first, find the right page or two, and you're all set. Again, this book isn't intended as summer-at-the-beach reading. It's mostly for looking up the kind of little facts and step-by-step procedures you're most likely to forget.

What Are These Parts?

The book is divided into eight parts plus some appendixes. The material in the appendixes is really the same kind of information that you find in the parts, but it doesn't fit the standard Quick Reference format.

Part I: Internet Basics for Mac Users

Although this book assumes that you probably got your basic Internet training from another IDG book, this is a brief run-through of the unique position of the Mac on the Internet.

Part II: E-Mail Essentials

The Internet is the world's biggest post office. These are the procedures for getting your e-mail addressed and sent correctly over the Net.

Part III: The World of Newsgroups

This part goes into the details of signing onto a newsgroup, scanning news without drowning in it, and finding groups that interest you.

Part IV: Archie and FTP

With Archie you find files, and with FTP you collect them. This covers the simplest and more advanced ways to use both utilities.

Part V: Gopher

Gopher actually folds most of the functions of Archie and FTP into a single program. This is a step-by-step exposition of Gopher use.

Part VI: The WWW and Mosaic

In a few years, most people will think of Mosaic and the Internet as synonymous. This part is an introduction to the world of the Web with a few simple procedures.

Part VII: Internet and On-Line Services

Most Mac users are likely to start out making Internet contact through a national service like CompuServe, so this part is a guide to what you get or don't get on each big service.

Part VIII: Business Resources

The business world of the Internet is the new Frontier, so this part gives you a rundown on current guideposts.

What the Little Icons Mean

You can do this task without consciously asserting any cogitation whatsoever.

You have to pay attention a bit when you try this procedure.

You can do the task (with the help of this Quick Reference!), but it will take some figuring.

Here's how you can find something on the Net — usually accompanied by an Internet address.

There's a potential problem that may not be obvious!

Don't forget the stuff marked by this icon!

When I offer a tip, it means I've tried everything else and this works best.

Points to other sections in this book where you can find more information.

More information is available in *The Internet For Macs For Dummies Starter Kit* by the same author!

Part 1

Internet Basics for Mac Users

What's the Internet?

Most computers in offices or universities can talk to each other over *networks,* which are just sets of wiring and software that let computers communicate with each other. The Internet provides a way for these computer networks to connect to other computer networks. If you want to contact people all over the world from your computer, the Internet is now the way to go.

The Internet lets you send files from one computer to another over a big, high-speed system of computer network connections that the U.S. Government paid for and installed. Because all these computers all over the planet can transfer files anywhere, *you* can have Internet access to any information that someone wants to place in the *public domain,* meaning that it's available to everyone with no restrictions. That's right: people actually develop programs and other valuable stuff and give them away. And a lot of it is really good! The next time someone cuts you off in traffic, tell yourself that it's probably someone hurrying home to post a free file just for you. And remember, files can be anything—besides software, you can have graphics files, poetry, supreme court decisions, scientific data, research material, song lyrics, library catalogues, or any other computer documents.

Combining all this information with electronic mail (e-mail) means the following:

- You can send messages to anyone across the Internet, and that person gets the messages right away.

- You can find thousands of useful files and free (!) programs.

- You can chat online with people *anywhere* (computer "chatting" is like CB radio).

- You can get all sorts of instant, up-to-date news.

Internet History

How did all this Internet stuff happen? In the 1970s, the Defense Department decided that research efforts would speed up if investigators with funding from the Advanced Research Projects Agency could communicate from one network to another. Usually, these networks were at big national labs such as Los Alamos or at universities such as MIT.

ARPANET, as this new setup was called, originally linked about 30 sites, most of which used computers that are now part of ancient history (Burroughs, Honeywell, and ancient DEC hardware). Some of the first ARPANET designers then were hired for another project that would let ARPANET connect to radio- and satellite-based computer communications. This effort defined the communication hardware and software that make an Internet connection.

In the 1980s, the old ARPA sites converted to Internet connection. Then the National Science Foundation (NSF) put together a high-speed network for Internet sites. Companies selling gateway hardware and software (a *gateway* is the actual connection from one network to another) for connecting to the NSF Net began to appear. Commercial Internet service networks were born. The whole package went from a few million users to more than 50 million, a figure growing even as you read this book.

Internet Reality

The original Internet system was designed for people who were comfortable with the Unix operating system. Unix is about as far from the Mac OS as you can get and still be talking about computers. In Unix, a relatively "friendly" utility for reading mail text files demands that you master a command set like the following:

```
& help
cd [directory]          chdir to directory or home if none given
d [message list]        delete messages
e [message list]        edit messages
f [message list]        show from lines of messages
h                       print out active message headers
m [user list]           mail to specific users
n                       goto and type next message
p [message list]        print messages
pre [message list]      make messages go back to system
mailbox
q                       quit, saving unresolved messages in mbox
r [message list]        reply to sender (only) of messages
s [message list] file   append messages to file
t [message list]        type messages (same as print)
top [message list]      show top lines of messages
u [message list]        undelete messages
v [message list]        edit messages with display editor
x                       quit, do not change system mailbox
z [-]                   display next [previous] page of headers
!                       shell escape
```

That was OK for the first two million users on the Internet, but it's not going to be the answer for the next 100 million, especially for those users who are comfortable only with a nice, graphical interface like the Mac's.

I'm telling you this so that you realize that Internet access is an area in rapid transition. Some basic Internet services, such as FTP, Gopher, Archie, and others, will stay fundamentally the same, but the way you access these services will change. This Quick Reference, for example, contains a whole chapter about the World Wide Web and Mosaic. In mid-1993, the World Wide Web was useful mostly to particle physicists, and only a few people outside the University of Illinois had even heard of Mosaic. The computer business changes ten times faster than the automobile industry, and the Internet changes ten times faster than the computer business!

E-Mail, Internet Addresses, and the @ Symbol

Some authorities estimate that the current Internet address system can handle 100 million international users without too much trouble. After that, experts have a proposal in place for a new address system that will accommodate many more people than could actually live on this small planet.

Internet addresses for e-mail are everywhere. If you look at a business card that belongs to someone in a high-tech business (or simply a large company), it's likely that one line on the card will give an e-mail address with an @ in it. That's how fast the technology moves — six years ago, most cards didn't even list a fax number.

For example, an Apple employee named Kermit T. Frog may have the following e-mail address:

```
kermitf@apple.com
```

The @ symbol is the tip-off that the address is an Internet-valid e-mail address; the notation . com means that the address is a business. (In this case, *com* is called the *Internet zone designation.*) When you read this address, you say "kermit eff at apple dot com." The @ in the address is pronounced *at* (just like the @ symbol on a keyboard).

Here's why addresses are important: If you have an @ address, you can communicate with anyone else on the planet with an @ address. That includes everyone who's anyone in the computer business and a large fraction of the people who are in charge of things at most organizations. To get taken seriously as a computer user or a businessperson in the next few years, you're going to need your own @ address.

For example, by 1994, you may be able to send a message to `vicepresident@whitehouse.gov` and help educate Al Gore on environmental issues ("Sir, I'd like to volunteer several distant states as nuclear waste dumps"). The zone designation `.gov` just means that the e-mail address is a government site. Professors at universities usually have addresses that end in `.edu`, for education, although sometimes an address indicates a location rather than a job category. I have an address at `well.sf.ca.us`, which just means that it's a bulletin board site called the WELL, near San Francisco, California, in the good old U.S. The following table lists some more examples:

Address	Interpretation
`@post.queensu.ca`	Queen's University in Canada (`.ca` at the end means Canada, while `.ca.us` is California)
`@coombs.anu.edu.au`	A research address at Australian National University
`@netcom.com`	A big commercial Internet service provider
`@nic.ddn.mil`	Internet info at a military site
`@aol.com`	America Online
`@whales.org`	A mythical nonprofit organization
`@nsf.net`	National Science Foundation network
`@unicef.int`	The code for international organizations
`@informatik.uni-hamburg.de`	Computer science department in Germany (Deutschland = `.de`)
`@leprechaun.ie`	Fantasy address in Ireland

I look at e-mail in detail in Part II. For now, all you need to know is that once you have an address with an @ in it, you're part of the Internet, at least from a connection point of view.

News, Gossip, and Chatter

A special feature of the Internet is the *newsgroup,* a sort of online discussion group about particular topics. Newsgroups actually started as a feature of a separate networking structure called USENET, but because nearly every USENET site was an Internet site and the Internet has engulfed all other public-domain networks anyway, people now just refer casually to "Internet newsgroups." Technology is, quite frankly, only a few months away from phase two of the Internet, in which the vast majority of

Internet users have never heard of USENET, BITNET, FidoNET, or other pioneers and are only dimly aware of the existence of Unix. That's all right — most computer users couldn't design a memory chip either and probably don't know who Robert Noyce is (he essentially invented the microprocessor).

Newsgroups, which are basically just specialized computer bulletin boards that you reach with Internet e-mail, demonstrate that the Internet isn't all science and business. Sure, it has resources on programming languages, and companies place catalogs on the Internet at the rate of hundreds of new projects per week, but it's also got lots of nonsense.

As one example, I regularly check comments from hundreds of people in the U.S. on the comedy TV program *Mystery Science Theater 3000*. This program has thousands of avid fans who chatter away on-line every day in a huge newsgroup. Because the particular specialty of *MST 3K* is obscure, funny references in wisecracks, a given remark on the show is capable of generating an endless stream of linked messages from fans explaining various perspectives on the original remark on the show. The same messaging characteristics apply to newsgroups on Macintosh hardware, but the messages aren't as funny.

The Internet's capability to connect files from all sorts of groups gives you a prime example of the persistence of human nature. Just as Middle Kingdom tombs in Egypt contain pornographic graffiti and the first artsy pictures of naked ladies followed the invention of photography by less than a year, it's a matter of record that two of the top ten most frequently accessed newsgroups are called `alt.sex` and `rec.arts.erotica`. This makes sense because a pretty big chunk of all the private computer bulletin boards out there specialize in adult material, and many of those boards are connected to the Net. Also, 85 percent of Internet users are male and their average age is 25, which may help to explain the phenomenal amount of bandwidth being chewed up in transmission of naughty bits.

Here's a sample of newsgroups and topics that you can investigate when you get connected:

Newsgroup	Topic
`comp.ai`	Artificial intelligence
`soc.culture.thai`	The latest from Bangkok and elsewhere
`sci.med.aids`	Current AIDS information
`alt.hotrod`	Souped-up vehicles, natch
`alt.rush-limbaugh`	Please note the hyphen

Newsgroup	Topic
alt.sport.baseball.chicago-cubs	Seminar on congenital optimism
talk.abortion	Abortion controversies of all kinds
rec.arts.poems	Write a poem, put it here
misc.answers	About Usenet itself
comp.sys.mac.wanted	Macs for sale

The Internet as a Reference Resource

As an Internet user with an @ address, you can exchange messages with other Internet users from Brazil to Baltimore. By itself, that capability makes the Internet extremely useful.

Besides communicating messages, the Internet can communicate files of information stored all over its many networks. The Library of Congress, for example, contains copies of all the books published in the United States and copies of nearly all magazines and newspapers ever published here. Although only 20,000 or so of the most useful books have been prepared for access as Internet files, several library groups are working to get the whole collection ready for the Internet.

The U.S. Patent Office has files for all the patents issued since it was founded. University libraries across the U.S. (Harvard, Yale, and the University of Illinois are the largest) have collections that represent all sorts of foreign research material not found even at the Library of Congress. All these collections, too, are being merrily scanned into a text-file format that your Macintosh can read (once your Macintosh gets the file from the Internet). Curiously, nowhere on the Internet is there an encyclopedia; they're all copyrighted. For that, you need one of the on-line services described in Part VII.

If you're sitting in front of your Macintosh, the Internet allows you to wander through the stacks in most of the libraries in the world. While you may not always be able to get individual books transferred to a library near you, the information in these books is steadily being converted to online files that you can download.

Getting Connected

If you're not on an Internet-connected network, you have to connect to the Internet by using your Mac and a modem. In traditional Internet access, this would mean that you could find a service provider and have either a shell account or a SLIP or PPP account. With a shell account, you use your Mac as a terminal to another bigger computer, and the bigger computer is really "on" the Internet. A Shell account is fire if you will mostly be sending text back and forth but most shell accounts aren't set up to handle graphics.

SLIP (Serial Line Internet Protocol) and the newer PPP (Point-to-Point Protocol) accounts give you a direct connection to the Internet, so you can use special Macintosh graphical software, such as Mosaic, MacWeb, and TurboGopher. In most cases, the disadvantage of a SLIP account is that you have to make an additional provision for e-mail because when you're not actually logged on and connected, some other computer has to hold your mail and forward it to you. See Appendix A for details on setting up your SLIP or connection.

Usually, you access a shell account with standard Mac communications software (some service providers have their own software). You need, therefore, to have some bits of information ready to fire up a shell account, as shown in these two dialog boxes from the popular program MicroPhone.

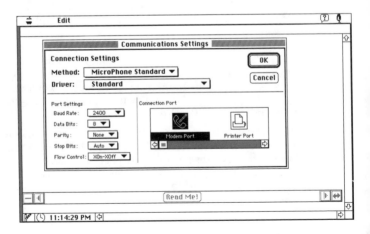

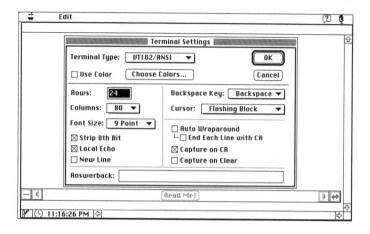

You need to know the following:

- **Your modem's maximum speed.** Surprisingly, some people whose Macs have built-in modems don't know this figure.

- **Data bits, parity, and stop bits for the service provider's protocol.** The service provider will tell you this information, although 8 data, None for parity, and auto for stop is a good first guess.

- **The service provider's phone number.** Usually, this will be a local access number on SprintNet or TymNet.

- **Local echo.** Some services GEnie, for example require that you set Local Echo in terminal settings.

Although some shell account providers have made an effort to spruce up the online interface, most e-mail on a shell account looks like the example in the next figure:

```
Path:search01.news.aol.com!newstf01.cr1.aol.com!uunet!MathWorks.Com!europa.eng.gt
efsd.com!library.ucla.edu!csulb.edu!csus.edu!netcom.com!zzz
From: zzz@netcom.com (Louis Zzizz)
Subject: Re: Mac Ftp Mirrors
Message-ID: <zzzCqFHpC.AoC@netcom.com>
References: <2s1fq9$f8c@news.CCIT.Arizona.EDU> <fujii-260594031300@ts7-
38.upenn.edu>
Date: Sun, 29 May 1994 21:15:11 GMT

Subject: Re: Mac Ftp Mirrors
From: zzz@netcom.com (Louis Zzizz)
Date: Sun, 29 May 1994 21:15:11 GMT
Message-ID: <zzzCqFHpC.AoC@netcom.com>

>> Where else can I ftp to get the Umich and/or Info-Mac files?

Here are two sites that are updated every day:

ftp.univie.ac.at      131.130.1.4     mac/info-mac          1/1
ftp.ucs.ubc.ca        137.82.27.62    pub/mac/info-mac      1/1

Louis Zziz        zzz@netcom.com      San Jose, CA
```

Mac users bought a Mac for straightforward point-and-click access to serious computer power, so you're probably looking for Internet access that follows a traditional Mac interface. That's created a demand for Internet e-mail on a service that looks a little better. Apple's own not-entirely-successful eWorld, for example, has e-mail that features document forms with clickable buttons and easy routing to the rest of the Internet, as the following figure shows.

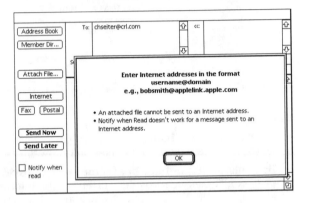

 Just now, there is no way to get full Internet access easily with a single software or service package, but some services are getting pretty close. America Online has been steadily plowing away and now offers Internet e-mail, newsgroups, Gopher searches, and FTP (file transfer protocol) for fetching files from remote computers. All these features are not only offered in a nice real-Mac interface, but, as this book goes to press, AOL is on the brink of implementing a World Wide Web graphical browser (see Part VI). When that appears, it's going to be hard to make a case for the traditional shell account from standard Internet service providers.

Another Internet service that's very close to offering a complete set of services is Pipeline. This service offers a nice dialog box format for the Internet utilities Archie and FTP (see Part IV).

In Pipeline FTP, you just fill in the name of the file you want and the site where it's located. The system handles the details, including transferring the file to your own computer from Pipeline's computer. Many Internet old-timers wouldn't agree with me (actually, many of them are dismayed at the barbarian hordes pouring through the wire), but I think that simpler interfaces like this are not just inevitable but better.

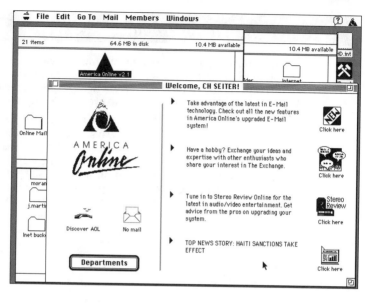

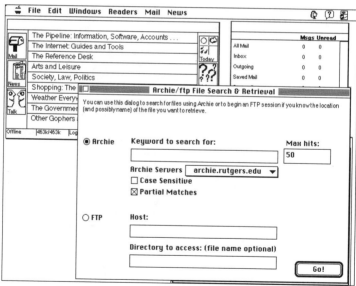

The Information Superhighway (WWW)

Remarkably, this expression spent only four or five months as ridiculous hype, and then a bunch of people miraculously built a sort of reality underneath it. For all practical purposes, the World Wide Web (WWW) is now what the expression *information superhighway* actually refers to.

You can to get to the WWW in three ways. The first is to accept a plain-text version of a WWW browser. This method isn't as much fun as the whole sound-plus-pictures version of the Web, but it does provide a great deal of information at speeds suited to modest (2400–9600 bps) modems. Here's a sample from the national on-line service Delphi, which doesn't yet have a "real-Mac" interface but provides complete Internet access:

```
WORLD WIDE WEB

Page 1 of 2


1     Type Any URL    WWW/Web

2     URL FAQ    Text

3     Britannica Online    WWW/Web

4     November Eclipse Information  WWW/Web

5     Global Network Navigator WWW/Web

6     Guide to Web Weavers      WWW/Web

7     EnviroWeb WWW/Web

8     Games Domain - Games related information site     WWW/Web

9     Guide to New Users by Steve Franklin    WWW/Web

10    Info from CERN WWW/Web

11    Infobot Hotlist Database WWW/Web

12    Interactive Employment Network    WWW/Web

13    Interesting Business Sites on the Web   WWW/Web

14    Internet Business Center WWW/Web

15    The InterNIC InfoGuide Home Page   WWW/Web

16    Library of Congress World Wide Web Home Page WWW/Web

17    NCSA Home Page WWW/Web

18    Plugged In (educational programs for low-income communities)

19    Random Site    WWW/Web


Enter Item Number, MORE, ?, or BACK: 11
```

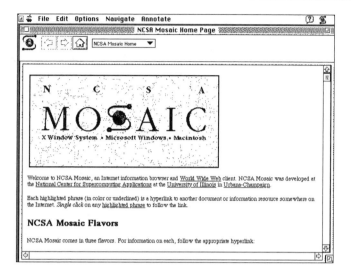

The second way is to get a SLIP account and download either NCSA Mosaic or MacWeb, the premier Web browsers from an FTP site (see Part VI). You'll not only get the hottest interface on the Net, which encourages you to roam the Net through links from one site and document to others, but you also get to hone in on the Net's main repositories of business information.

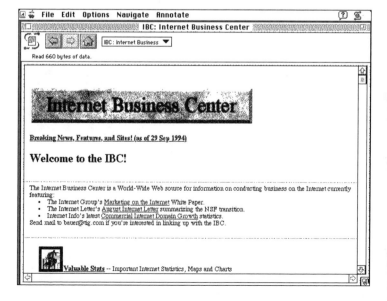

Another way to get these graphical benefits has recently surfaced in the form of a software fix-up that lets a shell account imper- sonate a SLIP account. It's called *The Internet Adapter* (TIA), and it's starting to revolutionize activities at traditional Internet shell account providers. At least one national on-line service is investigating using a modified version of TIA to provide real Mosaic on what's basically just an e-mail system. For more information, send e-mail to the company at `tia-sales@marketplace.com`.

Part II

E-Mail Essentials

With a Macintosh and a modem, you're connected to 50 to 100 million users of the Internet. If your Mac is on a network inside a business and the network has a modem, you can also send e-mail. Finally, if your Macintosh is directly connected to a network that itself is an Internet host (this is usually the case at universities), you don't even need the modem.

Understanding How E-Mail Works

When you send outgoing e-mail, your Internet service provider becomes the equivalent of the mailbox on the corner. You send a message to your pal Michael Nifty at `miken@world.com`. Your provider's mail decoder looks at the address of the recipient and routes it to the receiving Internet host, `world.com`. The receiving-end host acts like one of those big office mailbox systems with hundreds of pigeonholes. It finds `miken`, stores the message, and notifies him that he has new mail. Usually, he sees this notice the next time he logs on to the `world.com` system. Delivery is not instant, but it's certainly an improvement on any other system.

E-mail works as well as it does, in part, because the messages are primitive. This isn't multimedia — the e-mail messages I'm talking about are plain text, so messages can be created on any type of computer and read on any other type. And because they're just text, they're compact; a one-page color picture is a file 500 times bigger than a page of text. That makes a difference if you're using a relatively slow phone line (2400 bps) for Internet connection.

Extensions to the Internet mail system called MIME (for *m*ulti-media *I*nternet *m*ail *e*xtensions) are being implemented now at a variety of services. We should all hope that MIME really gets underway only when everyone has faster modems and faster computers, because the first versions of MIME-mail are going to result in an explosion in the sheer amount of gigabytes coursing through the Net.

Picking a Name

When you sign up with an Internet service provider — for example, Netcom (408-554-8649) — you get a local dial-up phone number and are asked to pick a name. Here's the story on Internet names: If your name is Steve Berlin, you can pick `Sberlin` as your Net name. That makes your Internet address `Sberlin@netcom.com`.

In Internet terminology, Netcom is the *host,* meaning a computer system with its own Internet numerical address. You, in turn, are a user attached to that host, but you are not a host yourself. Unless you get SLIP service (see Appendix A), you won't have an Internet number address (IP address) like 129.24.35.167.

You should take your choice of a name seriously. I don't know why, but Net directories are filled with silly names (winkie@aol.com) and first names (bill321@delphi.com). These types of names make you a lot harder to find through standard directory services. Do yourself a favor — pick a nice, dignified, businesslike name that makes you easy to trace. Honest, AEinstei, dfwilson, and rtmorgan will wear better over the years than stimpy52 or starman.

Sending Standard E-Mail

There are several better ways to use e-mail than the way I'm going to show you, but this simple way is really common. Some national on-line services have convenient and intuitive mail systems, and you can use a very nice, Macintosh-specific mail program called Eudora if you have a SLIP account (see Appendix A). But the typical Internet setup uses a plain-vanilla, Unix shell-account mail program like the one you see here.

1. To send a standard e-mail message, you need a standard communications program such as Z-Term (available for free) or Microphone LT (included with many modems).

2. You need to establish an account with a service provider. At this point every computer magazine lists several possible choices, especially the magazines *Boardwatch* and *Online Access.*

3. To log on to your system, you need your name, your password, and the service phone number (typically, a local SprintNet number).

4. After you log on, you get a prompt. One common prompt is the % symbol. That's right, to assist you in figuring out what to do next, the big, Unix-based Internet computer sends you the percent sign.

5. In most Unix shells, this starts the mail program. At the prompt, you can type **mail president@whitehouse.gov**.

By the way, if you find yourself stuck using this kind of interface, at the % prompt you can also type **man**, or in some systems, **help**, and the main system typically gives you a choice of selections from the operating systems manual.

The system responds with this:

```
mail president@whitehouse.gov
Subject:
```

6. Enter a subject name and press Return. Type your message (this sample is just for fun):

```
mail president@whitehouse.gov
Subject: Sorry About That, Chief


Please don't take the recent election re-
sults so hard. Twenty years of declining
real incomes have put the voters in a sur-
real mood. Better luck next time.


Yours sincerely,
Steve Berlin (you know, the musician from LA)
```

7. To send the message, press Ctrl-D (hold down Ctrl and D at the same time).

In some other systems, command is Ctrl-Z.

The system sends you EOT, signifying "end of transmission."

E-Mail Tips

Some of these tips may seem obvious, but they seem to have escaped the attention of many experienced Internet users.

- The best way to find someone's address is simply to ask for it over the phone. Sometimes you can even state your message.

  If that tip fails, try IDG Books' *Internet White Pages,* which lists names and e-mail addresses.

- DON'T USE CAPITAL LETTERS IN MESSAGES.

- In plain-text e-mail, it's hard to tell when you're kidding. Be funny in person and straightforward in e-mail, you lamentable buffoon (just kidding).

- Make sure that the person receiving the message can tell who you are. Always put your actual name and phone number in the body of your message.

Some messages from one network to another appear with the first network as the sender, instead of you.

- Put **?** first in the subject line of unsolicited messages, as in *?are you the Fred Layne who went to high school in Auburn, CA?*

More E-Mail Hints

Here are a few more points to keep in mind.

- Your message will arrive with a header that contains all sorts of system information. If you're curious, the header lets you trace the complicated route of your message through the Internet's computers.

```
Path:search01.news.aol.com!newstf01.cr1.aol.com!uunet!MathWorks.Com!europa.eng.gt
efsd.com!library.ucla.edu!csulb.edu!csus.edu!netcom.com!zzz
From: zzz@netcom.com (Louis Zzizz)
Subject: Re: Mac Ftp Mirrors
Message-ID: <zzzCqFHpC.AoC@netcom.com>
References: <2s1fq9$f8c@news.CCIT.Arizona.EDU> <fujii-260594031300@ts7-
38.upenn.edu>
Date: Sun, 29 May 1994 21:15:11 GMT

Subject: Re: Mac Ftp Mirrors
From: zzz@netcom.com (Louis Zzizz)
Date: Sun, 29 May 1994 21:15:11 GMT
Message-ID: <zzzCqFHpC.AoC@netcom.com>

>> Where else can I ftp to get the Umich and/or Info-Mac files?

Here are two sites that are updated every day:

ftp.univie.ac.at     131.130.1.4     mac/info-mac      1/1
ftp.ucs.ubc.ca       137.82.27.62    pub/mac/info-mac   1/1

Louis Zziz        zzz@netcom.com      San Jose, CA
```

- If you make a mistake in the address, even the simplest typo, the message won't get through. In some systems, after a brief delay you are told that the address isn't working. Typically, however, the message goes out on the Internet and gets bounced back to you later; you'll find it returned the next time you connect to your host system. It's critical to get an Internet address exactly right. Unlike the Post Office, the Internet has no way to guess around your typos.

- Some Unix-based hosts feature a mailing system called *elm*. This program has a nice repertoire of commands and a full screen editor. Try typing **elm** at the system prompt and see whether you get a response. It beats composing mail in a line editor.

Finding Better E-Mail Systems

There are, of course, several systems for e-mail that are better that what you'll find in a simple shell account.

- Some service providers have menu-driven systems, where you don't have to keep a set of commands in mind. This system makes help available at all times.

```
                  COMMAND OPTIONS FOR USING EMAIL

mail userid  ...Send email to another WELL user.  You will be prompted for
             a "Subject".  Type a short subject header and hit Return.
             Then, enter the text of your message, hitting Return at
             the end of each line (about 70 chars wide).  To abandon
             the message without sending it, hit control-c twice.

             To send the letter, go to a new line, type a dot (.),
             and hit Return.

mail         ...Read your mail.  You will see a list of your mail items
             and a prompt which looks like this:  &   ...To read each
             consecutive mail item, hit Return at this "&" prompt.

             Type: r    ...to respond to the current message.

             Type: dt   ...to delete the current message.

             Type: q    ...to quit email.
```

- All the national on-line services have e-mail services that are vastly superior to the old Unix mail system in terms of convenience (actually, they are the Unix system, but with a better front end).

Compare the following two figures. In my opinion, they present an unarguable case for national services over shell accounts. Both Delphi and AOL offer lots of free trial time to investigate their services, and either one is worth considering. (Delphi is for more hard-core Internet fans, while AOL is for Mac users who want to take it easy). Make your own decision, but contact me at chseiter@aol.com if you can think of a reason not to try one of the services in Part VII.

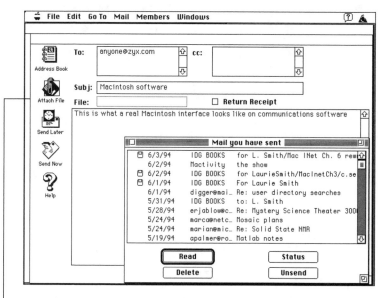

```
Sun Mar 13 23:50:20 PST 1994
crl1% mail
Mail version SMI 4.0 Fri Jul 2 11:55:02 PDT 1993 Type ? for help.
"/usr/spool/mail/chseiter": 1 message 1 new
>N 1 wilson       Sat Mar 12 26 05:59  36/1103 Macworld note

& mail chseiter@aol.com
Subject: comm1
Hi. If you can read this, you're not having fun.
.
EOT

New mail has arrived.
crl2% mail
Mail version SMI 4.0 Fri Jul 2 11:55:02 PDT 1993 Type ? for help.
"/usr/spool/mail/chseiter": 1 message 1 new
>N 1 MAILER-DAEMON  Sun Mar 13 23:53  24/719
Returned mail: User unknown
& d 1
& quit
|
```

The traditional Internet mail interface.

Internet mail meets the Macintosh.

Internet Number Addresses

Internet hosts have machine addresses composed of four numbers separated by dots. Thus, the WELL in San Francisco is called `well.sf.ca.us`, but the other Internet machines know it as `198.93.4.10`.

The numbers between the dots range from 1 to 254. That means that there are $254 \times 254 \times 254 \times 254$ possible addresses — the number is about 4 billion.

You can assign the network address in different ways, so the people who assigned them made up three classes: A, B, and C. Class A networks can support about 16 million hosts. Class C networks can handle 254 hosts. Because a host computer on a network can handle several incoming lines, there's a lot of room out there.

Inside a big network, a method called subnetting simplifies addressing from one network to the next, and another method called supernetting lets organizations effectively address several smaller networks as if they were one big network.

Sample E-Mail Address Formats

The national on-line services (see Part VII) occasionally have some funny wrinkles in their addresses and user IDs. CompuServe and Prodigy users have cryptic names, and GEnie isn't just called GEnie in its Internet address. Here's a quick reference to the most common addresses. Note particularly that the comma in the normal CompuServe address has been changed to a period for Internet mail.

To Send To	With This Address	Use This Address
AOL	Bob Wilson	bobwilson@aol.com
CompuServe	70340,701	70340.701 @compuserve.com
Delphi	bwilson	bwilson@delphi.com
eWorld	Bob Wilson	bobwilson@eworld.com
GEnie	WILSON318	WILSON318@ genie.geis.com
Prodigy	HBNM07A	HBNM07A.prodigy.com

Part III

The World of Newsgroups

Newsgroups are a big part of the fascination of the Internet. Strictly speaking, newsgroups are the domain of USENET, which is not exactly part of the Internet. USENET is a protocol for exchanging computer bulletin boards of messages on specific topics among computers — one computer makes up a current list of messages and forwards it to others, which in turn forwards it to still others.

Essentially, all the computers involved in this service are on the Internet, so the newsgroups (bulletin boards) are perceived by nearly everyone as Internet functions.

What's a Newsgroup?

It's easier to explain this term with examples than with a definition. There's a newsgroup called `comp.sys.mac.misc` that's full of messages about Macintoshes in general. A newsgroup called `alt.antiques` is a sort of computer classified ad system. The newsgroup called `alt.tv.x-files` amounts to a user-contributed fan-club newsletter for the Fox network's TV show *The X Files*. USENET newsgroups (see Appendix C) not only cover every area of human interest and behavior, but they also cover all sorts of areas I can't even print in this book. It's a big world out there — some people collect antique scientific instruments, and some people do jaw-droppingly kinky stuff with their neighbors.

In every case, the newsgroup consists of sets of messages called *threads*, which start with an original message and continue with the trail of comments to the original message. Newsgroups are arranged in *hierarchies*, which is why their names have little dot structures like Internet addresses do. Here's a listing of top-level (first part of the name) newsgroups available on one service (the Well in San Francisco).

```
------------------------  ACTIVE NEWSGROUPS  ------------------------
                TOP Level Group Categories:
---------------------------------------------------------------------

    1. alt.              15. gnu.             29. talk.
    2. ba.               16. hiv.             30. test
    3. bionet.           17. ieee.            31. to.
    4. bit.              18. info.            32. trial.
    5. biz.              19. k12.             33. u3b.
    6. ca.               20. magic.           34. ua.
    7. comp.             21. misc.            35. uk.
    8. control           22. nbn.             36. vmsnet.
    9. courts.           23. ncar.            37. za.
   10. ddn.              24. news.
   11. eunet.            25. nm.
   12. fr.               26. rec.
   13. general           27. sci.
   14. geometry.         28. soc.
```

Each one of these top levels has other levels below it (alt. alone has thousands). Not every service carries every newsgroup—for reasons of lack of interest, raunchiness, or lack of space, services usually offer a big subset of all possible newsgroups but not the whole show.

Besides containing lots of useful information, newsgroups are really where the *fun* is on the Internet. The following sections look at different kinds of newsgroup access.

See *The Internet For Macs For Dummies* for more information on newsgroups.

Newsgroups with NN

This old-time Unix religion is found on many services, from bulletin boards to shell accounts to Delphi. The newsreader utility NN, a standard Unix method to get access to newsgroups, is much harder to use than modern interfaces, but it's efficient and powerful. Here's how you look at news postings in this basic system.

1. For typical access, type **USENET** at the system prompt.

```
About the Internet      FTP-File Transfer Protocol
Conference              Gopher
Databases (Files)       IRC-Internet Relay Chat
EMail                   Telnet
Forum (Messages)        Utilities (finger, traceroute, ping)
Guides (Books)          Usenet Newsgroups
Register/Cancel
Who's Here              Help
Workspace               Exit

Internet SIG>Enter your selection: usenet

USENET Menu:

About Usenet Discussion Groups
Usenet (Delphi Newsreader)
NN Newsreader (Usenet)
Instructions for the NN Newsreader
Exit

USENET>Enter your selection: usenet
```

That gets you (at least in nonprimitive services) to a numbered menu that lists USENET options. Most services keep some favorite newsgroups ready in this menu and offer you the opportunity to assign any newsgroup to your account on the service (choice 2 in the first figure on the next page).

2. Select one of the newsgroups by number.

You see a listing of message threads (second figure, next page). Then you can select one of the threads by letter.

```
Usenet Discussion Groups

1    PERSONAL FAVORITES                                          Menu
2    Access Any Newsgroup (by typing its name)                  Usenet
3    HELP FILES and FAQs!                                        Menu
4    Searchable Lists of Newsgroups and Mailing Lists           Menu
5                                                                Text
6    ===================SELECTED NEWSGROUPS===================   Text
7    READ BEFORE POSTING TO ANY NEWSGROUP!!!!                    Text
8    Haiti Events (alt.current-events.haiti)                     Usenet
9    Best of Internet--DON'T POST!See FAQ (alt.best.of.internet) Usenet
10   Comet Shoemaker-Levy 9 (alt.sl9)                            Usenet
11   Commercial Online Services (alt.online-service)            Usenet
12   Computer Underground Digest (comp.society.cu-digest)        Usenet
        **(list break here)***
29   News Answers (news.answers)                                 Usenet
30   Newsgroup Questions (news.groups.questions)                Usenet
31   Newsgroup Reviews (news.groups.reviews)                    Usenet
32   Newsgroups (news.groups)                                    Usenet
33   News Lists (news.lists)                                     Usenet
34   Proposals for New Alt groups (alt.config)                  Usenet
35   Puzzles (rec.puzzles)                                       Usenet
36   Urban Folklore (alt.folklore.urban)                        Usenet
37   Wired Magazine (alt.wired)                                  Usenet
38   Test Group (misc.test)                                      Usenet
```

```
a  lara@sgi.c    1341        Textiles FAQ
b  Rob Miracle    567        Key West, FL - Frequently Asked Questions w/answers
c  lara@sgi.sgi.co 741       Textile Related Books FAQ: Part 2 of 2
d  Piet          1718        Computer Music bibliography
e  Piet           327        Midi files/software archives on the Internet
f  Evan Koffler  1084        alt.games.gb Frequently A<>d Questions (Part 1 of 2)
g  Bob           1649        FAQ - ASCII Art Questions & Answers (4.6 - 56 K)
h  Scott A. Yanof 1401 [3]   Updated Internet Services List
i  Scott A. Yanoff 890       Updated Inter-Network Mail Guide
j  SCOTT I CHASE 1474        Sci.Physics Frequently As<>ons (1/4) - Administrivia
k  SCOTT I CHASE 1364        Sci.Physics Frequently As<> - Cosmology/Astrophysics
l  SCOTT I CHASE 1131        Sci.Physics Frequently As<>s (3/4) - General Physics
m  SCOTT I CHASE 1105        Sci.Physics Frequently As<>4) - Particles/SR/Quantum
n  Mike           887        alt.fan.dave_barry Frequently Asked Questions
o  Arthur         327        >alt.sex.wanted FAQ
p  Helen T Rose   325        IRC Frequently Asked Questions (FAQ)
q  Jef Poskanzer  176        (30oct94) Welcome to alt.<>tils - automated posting.
r  Keith          451        Sushi (Japanese Cuisine) <>you mean it's not cooked?
s  Keith          154        Sushi (Japanese Cuisine) <>, that's not minute rice!
```

3. Press the letter of the thread you want to select.

Once you're reading the messages in a thread, NN gives you lots of choices. The problem is, you're unlikely to remember them unless you use NN a lot.

```
SELECT (toggle)                      MOVE
a-z0-9  Specified article            ,         Next menu line
x-y     Range x to y                 /         Previous menu line
x*      Same subject as x            SPACE     Next menu page (if any)
        Current article              < >       Prev/Next menu page
@ ~     Reverse/Undo all selections  ^ $       First/Last menu page
=regexp Matching subjects (=. selects all)
L/JJJJ  Leave/Change attributes
SHOW SELECTED ARTICLES
SPACE   Show (only when on last menu page)
Z       Show NOW, and return to this group afterwards
X       Show NOW, and continue with next group
GOTO OTHER GROUPS
X       Update current group, skip to next.    Y    Group overview
N P     Goto next/previous group.              ~/.nn/init:
G       Goto named group or open a folder.          Defines group
B A     Go back/forward in groups already read.     presentation sequence.
MISCELLANEOUS
U C     (Un)subscribe / Cancel                 :man    Online manual
F R M   Follow-up/Reply/Mail                   :help   More online help
S O W   Save articles                          !       Shell escape
:post   Post new article                       ~       Change menu layout
:unshar :decode :patch  Unpack articles        Q       Quit nn
Hit any key to continue
```

I recommend invoking the on-line manual and investigating the kill command in NN. This powerful command lets you automatically avoid reading messages by someone you have determined is a jerk or avoid boring threads. Kill is your reward for putting up with this interface.

Newsgroups with On-line Services: CompuServe

An on-line service can take the basic structure of NN and turn it into a simple command menu that you have present at all times. You lose some efficiency but gain in convenience.

This example shows you how you access newsgroups on a service that presents you with a menu system, instead of relying on your memory or a cheat sheet.

1. In the plain CompuServe interface (not CompuServe Information Manager), choose USENET from the starting menu when you sign on the service.

   The USENET interface gives you a basic repertoire of access actions.

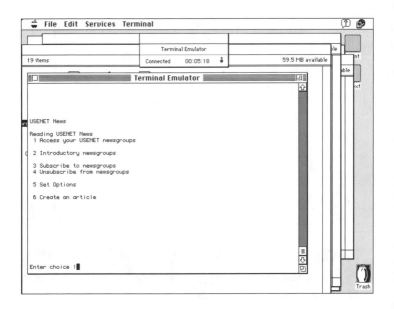

The newsreader actions in the CompuServe menu are simple choices that cover most of the same commands available in NN (sorry, no kill action, though).

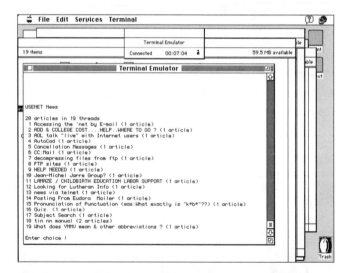

```
USENET News

Choices
 1 REPLY
 2 REPLY with Quotation
 3 MAIL
 4 CREATE an article
 5 CANCEL article

 6 REREAD this article
 7 HOLD this article
 8 NEXT article
 9 NEXT THREAD
10 PARENT article

11 CLEAR articles in this newsgroup
12 IGNORE
13 DOWNLOAD this article




Enter choice !
```

2. Select the option Subscribe to newsgroups at the starting USENET screen.

   You get the set of choices in the preceding figure. Following by-the-numbers menu, CompuServe takes you into the newsgroup threads with the options in the following figure.

```
 File  Edit  Services  Terminal                              (?) (%)

┌─────────────────────────────────────────────────────────────┐
│                      Terminal Emulator                       │
│ 19 items          Connected   00:07:04       59.5 MB available│
│  ════════════════════ Terminal Emulator ════════════════════ │
│                                                               │
│                                                               │
│  USENET News                                                  │
│                                                               │
│  20 articles in 19 threads                                    │
│   1 Accessing the 'net by E-mail (1 article)                  │
│   2 ADD & COLLEGE COST....HELP..WHERE TO GO ? (1 article)     │
│   3 AOL talk "live" with Internet users (1 article)           │
│   4 AutoCad (1 article)                                       │
│   5 Cancellation Messages (1 article)                         │
│   6 CC:Mail (1 article)                                       │
│   7 decompressing files from ftp (1 article)                  │
│   8 FTP sites (1 article)                                     │
│   9 HELP NEEDED (1 article)                                   │
│  10 Jean-Michel Jarre Group? (1 article)                      │
│  11 LAMAZE / CHILDBIRTH EDUCATION LABOR SUPPORT (1 article)   │
│  12 Looking for Lutheran Info (1 article)                     │
│  13 news via telnet (1 article)                               │
│  14 Posting From Eudora  Mailer (1 article)                   │
│  15 Pronunciation of Punctuation (was:What exactly is "k*b*"??) (1 article) │
│  16 Quiz. (1 article)                                         │
│  17 Subject Search (1 article)                                │
│  18 tin nn manual (2 articles)                                │
│  19 What does YMMV mean & other abbreviations ? (1 article)   │
│                                                               │
│  Enter choice !                                               │
└─────────────────────────────────────────────────────────────┘
                                                          Trash
```

Newsgroups with On-line Services: America Online, Pipeline, and Prodigy

It's about time for a no-brains-whatsoever approach to newsgroup reading. I'll show you three examples here, taken from the national on-line services America Online and Prodigy and the special Internet service Pipeline.

For more information on on-line services, see *The Internet For Macs For Dummies Starter Kit*.

America Online

The ultimate in simplicity is probably America Online's newsgroup interface, a carefully planned service that's the ultimate in "empty tank" navigation. One simple screen (reach it with the keyword Internet in the Go To menu at the welcome screen) gives you access to any newsgroup, and you manage your selected newsgroups in the Read My Newsgroups window (click to this window from the Newsgroups screen).

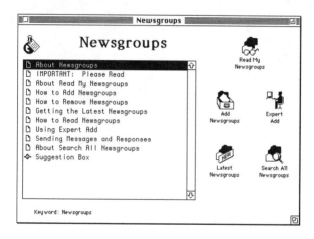

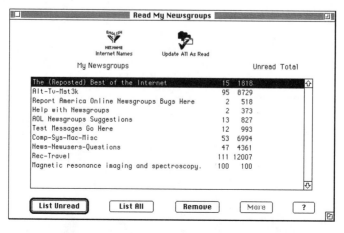

In my humble opinion, the newsgroup service alone makes it worth subscribing to AOL.

Pipeline

1. Find the choice called News Folders under the menu item News in Pipeline.

2. Give yourself a new folder by clicking that button.

3. Choose Edit Folder for your new folder.

   Pipeline then presents you with a list and lets you pick the newsgroups you find interesting.

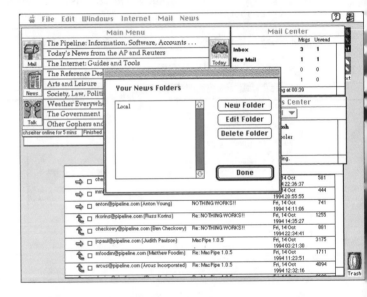

4. If you know the name of the groups you want, you can add groups one at a time. Otherwise, you can pull down the Categories list or first filter the whole set of newsgroups (including only groups that start with *sci,* for example) using the Filter option.

The Categories choice lets you look at the elements of the top domains and select groups one at a time or in batches. You don't have to know any newsgroup names in advance (unlike the situation with the NN reader or with CompuServe).

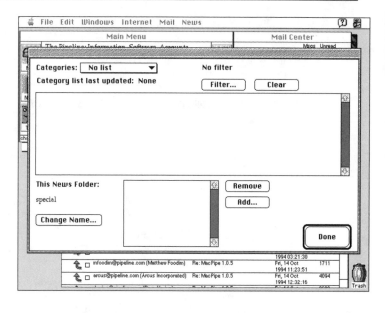

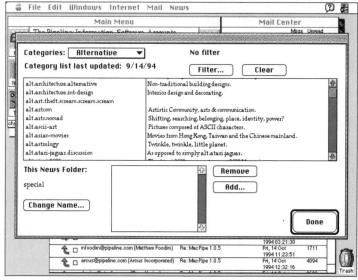

5. To add a newsgroup so that Pipeline has the messages ready in your folder when you sign on, just click any newsgroup name and then click the Add button.

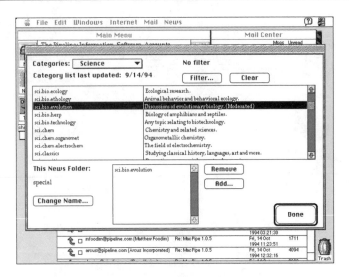

In a newsgroup message listing on Pipeline, you see individual messages with straight arrows (meaning first message in a thread) and curved arrows (meaning responses).

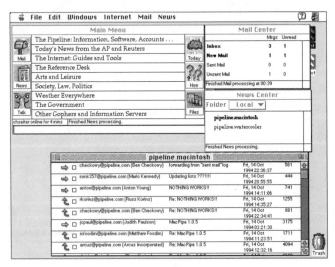

When you open a message, Pipeline treats it as just another piece of e-mail, except that the service retains the newsgroup name as the mailing address for responses. The great advantage of bringing newsgroup access into a Mac interface is that you can edit your replies with a TeachText-style editor, which is light years ahead of Unix line editors.

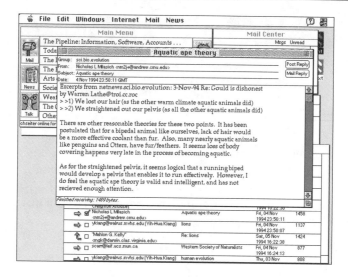

Prodigy

A graphical, menu-driven interface greatly simplifies adding and removing newsgroups from your personal list. Even Prodigy, a service with the gravest trepidation about the Internet and its nasty newsgroups, has finally added a point-and-click newsgroup interface in its latest software version.

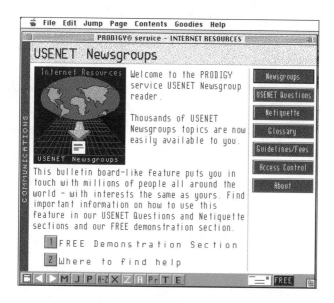

Newsgroups with a SLIP Connection

If you have a SLIP service provider and have installed MacTCP
and InterSLIP, you can use the freeware Macintosh newsreader
program called Nuntius, available in the software download area
of every on-line service.

If you're a serious news fanatic, you'll want this program. It allows
you to process news faster than you can do it on the slightly more
convenient national services. Here's how to use it:

1. Make a SLIP connection and double-click Nuntius.

   The first time you connect to your SLIP service, it downloads a list of all the newsgroups available for that server.

(For more information on making a SLIP connection, see
Appendix A.)

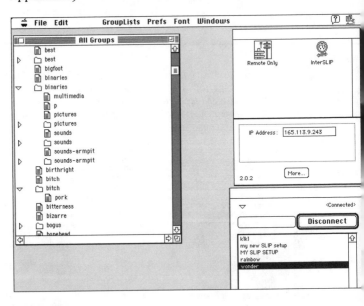

2. Double-click the folders and documents you're interested
   in, just as if the information were resident on your own Mac
   already.

   The threads appear in straightforward lists, so you
   shouldn't have any trouble.

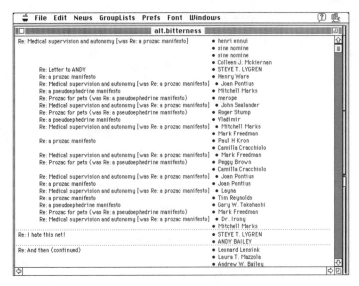

3. To open a message in a thread, just double-click its title.

   In Nuntius, you can pick your own favorite text editor (the first following figure), control the connection parameters to your service provider (the second following figure), and control the display of threads (the third following figure) so that you can filter out older material or threads you've already read.

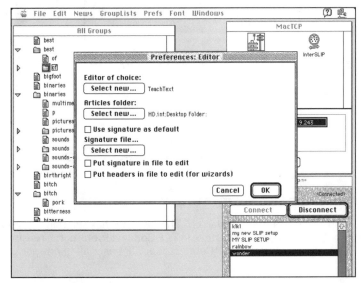

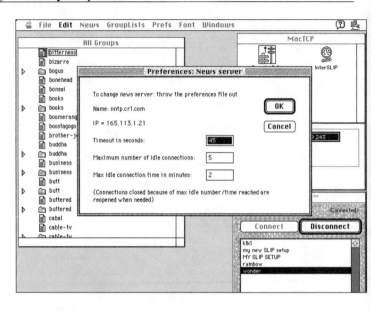

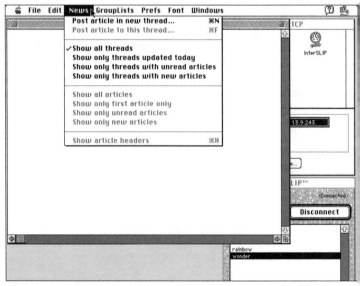

Pretty spectacular, eh? This interface has been carefully imitated in the News interface in TCP Connect II, one of the reasons I recommend TCP Connect as a SLIP-based all-in-one package.

Part IV

Archie and FTP

In the traditional world of the Internet, you find files on other computers by using a Unix program called Archie and then recover them to your own computer with the file transfer protocol (FTP), which is embodied, naturally enough, in a utility called FTP.

Presumably, you are reading this book because you have a Macintosh. That means that I can give you a frank opinion. The opinion is: the old way stinks. I'm going to go through file searching and retrieval step-by-step with a strong prejudice in favor of slick, new Mac software, as opposed to old-time Unix utilities. The old Unix way did have the advantages that it was especially thrifty with computing resources and that it could operate with nearly any computer. These virtues, however, don't matter quite so much in a world where the only mainstream desktop computers are fast Macs and Windows boxes with scads of memory.

Archie

Archie, in its classic form, is just a search utility that looks for titles of files on remote computers. What makes it useful is that it's set up to search file *archives,* so you simply set Archie to work on a special computer (a server) that maintains a list of all the files on Internet-connected computers. You send out some simple commands, and you get back a list of the locations of the files you're trying to find.

Anarchie, a Real Mac Program

(Just so you don't sound naive to Mac hipsters, this program name is pronounced *anarchy,* not *an archie.*) If you have a SLIP connection (see Appendix A), you can use the shareware program Anarchie, which is available from user groups, from most national on-line services (America Online, CompuServe, and others), and from Pipeline. Anarchie isn't completely a snap (it's still a sort of front end for the Unix commands), but it deals with folders and files in the familiar Macintosh style.

1. Make a SLIP connection to your Internet SLIP service provider with InterSLIP.

2. Find your copy of Anarchie and simply double-click the application icon.

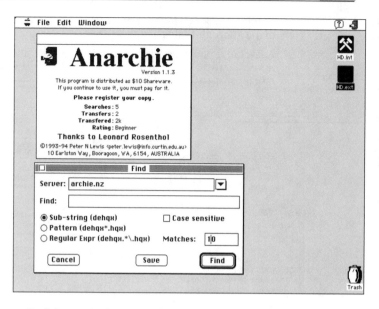

3. Select an Archie server that is working at an off-peak time. (You can try to get on during prime time, but it won't often work.)

Anarchie gives you its own scrolling list. Consult your wristwatch and a globe and pick an Archie server that's at 5 a.m. local time—that's the best way to avoid a busy signal.

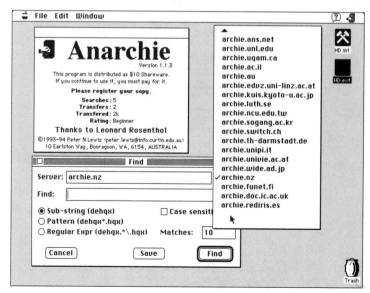

4. Enter the program name or name fragment in the Find field of the Anarchie dialog box.

Anarchie supports regular-expression searches, but frankly, it's easier to do simple searches in Anarchie and leave the fancier stuff to Gopher (Part V).

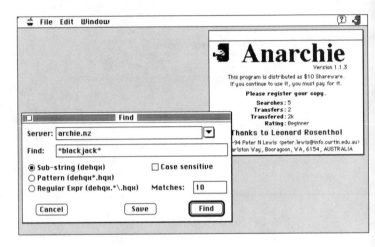

5. When Anarchie returns its search results, it presents them as folders. Double-click these folders to open them and then inspect the search results.

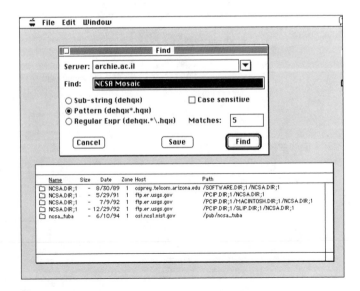

Archie, Basic Version

Most of the versions of Archie that rely on terminal-style programs — the simplest kind of communications software — work
approximately the same way.

1. Before you start, look up an Archie site.

   See "Archie, Text Menu Version" for an example of a list.

2. At the system prompt, type **telnet**.

```
About the Internet    FTP-File Transfer Protocol
Conference            Gopher
Databases (Files)     IRC-Internet Relay Chat
EMail                 Telnet
Forum (Messages)      Utilities (finger, traceroute, ping)
Guides (Books)        Usenet Newsgroups
Register/Cancel
Who's Here            Help
Workspace             Exit

Internet SIG>Enter your selection: telnet


Enter INTERNET address: archie.ac.il
|Telnet| Open
Trying shuldig.cs.huji.ac.il,telnet (132.65.16.8,23) ...
Escape (attention) character is "^\"

SunOS UNIX (shuldig)

login: archie
archie
# Message of the day from the localhost Prospero server:

                      Welcome to Archie!
                        Version 3.2
```

3. At the system prompt, enter an Internet address, which in
   this case is an Archie address.

   The address I'm using for this experiment is archie.ac.il.

4. After some messages from the remote system, you're
   prompted to log in.

5. Log in as **archie**.

   Use lowercase because you are logging into a Unix system,
   which typically uses only lowercase commands.

6. With any luck, you will find yourself in a system that gives
   you at least some help with its Archie implementation.

Before you run Archie, you should be aware that the huge size of
the Internet makes some precautions necessary. If you tell Archie
to find every file that has the word *mac* in the title, Archie will run
away for hours and come back with unmanageable piles of files.
You have three ways around this problem:

- If you enter the exact name of a file, the search is narrowed.

- If you want to learn how to impose logical limits on a search, you can usually type man archie and get back a text file that will introduce you to the wonders of "regular expressions" in Unix.

- A best bet is to limit the maximum number of hits you want reported.

  In the following figure, I set the maximum number of hits to 5, just to get the search over in hurry.

The simplest command that you can use to find some file information is *prog,* as in prog NCSA Mosaic.

```
                      Welcome to Archie!
                         Version 3.2

# Bunyip Information Systems, 1993, 1994

# Terminal type set to `vt100 24 80'.
# `erase' character is `^?'.
# `search' (type string) has the value `sub'.

archie.ac.il> set maxhits 5
set maxhits 5
archie.ac.il> prog NCSA Mosaic
prog NCSA Mosaic
# Search type: sub.
# Your queue position: 1
# Estimated time for completion: 10 seconds.
=

Host ftp.er.usgs.gov    (130.118.4.2)
Last updated 06:37  1 Nov 1994


   Location: /PCIP.DIR;1/MACINTOSH.DIR;1
      DIRECTORY    d-----x-w-      1 bytes  20:01  9 Jul 1992  NCSA.DIR;1
```

The prog instruction produces a grab bag of files, some of which have NCSA in their name and some of which have Mosaic itself. The first search hit for my example is in the following FTP site:

    ftp.er.usgs.gov

If you want to investigate the NCSA files there, you need that name as an input to the FTP utility.

Archie, Text Menu Version

The difficulty with using stock classic Archie is that you have to know where you're going and you have to know what you want. That's not always the case. Fortunately, if you are using a service provider that makes any concessions to new Internet users, you are likely to find at least some kind of Archie menu, as opposed to raw telnet Archie.

Usually, an Archie menu can be found under a listing of search facilities. If the listing doesn't appear at your system's top menu level, type **help search** at the system prompt.

When you find such a menu, here's what to do:

1. Click the Archie choice.

```
Selection 16 = SEARCH UTILITIES

1    Archie--Search for files at FTP Sites          Menu
2    Find People (KIS, NETFIND, Phonebooks, Usenet, WHOIS)  Menu
3    Find 800 Phone Numbers (AT&T)                  WWW/Web
4    Gophers by Subject Area (from RiceInfo, Rice Univ.)  Menu
5    HYTELNET 6.6: connect to libraries, BBS, CWIS, etc.  Menu
6    The Internet Prospector (Bunyip)               Menu
7    Jughead: Search directory titles in Gopherspace  Search
8    NETINFO: Find IP addresses, domain names       Telnet
9    Netmailsites: find sites                       Telnet
10   Search for Mailing Lists and Newsgroups        Menu
11   Usenet FAQs                                    Menu
12   VERONICA- Search titles in Gopherspace         Menu
13   WAIS                                           Menu
14   WWW Subject Search Guides                      Menu
```

You see a set of possible Archie sites.

In the following figure, the second field — the telnet field — means that you'll be dealing with a menu at another computer, whereas the search field indicates that your host system maintains a search menu.

```
Archie--Search for files at FTP Sites
Page 1 of 1

1    Archie at InterNIC                    Telnet
2    Archie at InterNIC (alternate 1)      Telnet
3    Archie at InterNIC (alternate 2)      Telnet
4    Dynamic Archie at InterNIC by WAIS    Search
5    Archie at ANS                         Telnet
6    Archie at Rutgers                     Telnet
7    Archie Quick Instructions             Text
8    Archie Full Instructions              Text
```

2. If you select the InterNIC/WAIS Archie server, you see the simple directive Search For:, which is followed by other instructions if the server is available.

   If you select an Archie server with a telnet field, you're back to the situation in the preceding section on Basic Version instructions.

```
Archie--Search for files at FTP Sites
Page 1 of 1

1    Archie at InterNIC                    Telnet
2    Archie at InterNIC (alternate 1)      Telnet
3    Archie at InterNIC (alternate 2)      Telnet
4    Dynamic Archie at InterNIC by WAIS    Search
5    Archie at ANS                         Telnet
6    Archie at Rutgers                     Telnet
7    Archie Quick Instructions             Text
8    Archie Full Instructions              Text

Enter Item Number, SAVE, ?, or BACK: 4

"Dynamic Archie at InterNIC by WAIS" is an indexed service.
Please specify a word or words to search.

Search for: ncsa mosaic
```

There is, however, a bit of trouble in paradise. Although Archie is pretty efficient, it does call a direct telnet line from you into the remote computer, which often gets you a busy signal.

```
6    Archie at Rutgers                     Telnet

Please log in as: archie

|Telnet| Open
Trying dorm.Rutgers.EDU,0 (128.6.18.15,0) ...

SunOS UNIX (dorm.rutgers.edu) (ttyr3)

login: archie
archie
Last login: Sun Nov  6 19:37:18 from sun26.cs.wisc.ed
SunOS Release 4.1.3 (TDSERVER-SUN4C) #2: Mon Jul 19 18:37:02 EDT 1993

ALL ARCHIE SESSIONS IN USE

I'm sorry. This archie server is currently at the limit of its
interactive login sessions. Please use another archie server or try
again |later.
```

When this happens, consult your wristwatch and a globe and pick an Archie server that's at 5 a.m. local time. Getting your advice on files from servers in Korea and Finland may seem strange, but at the right times of day those servers are the answer to your prayers.

```
List of active archie servers

  archie.au                    139.130.4.6      Australia
  archie.edvz.uni-linz.ac.at   140.78.3.8       Austria
  archie.univie.ac.at          131.130.1.23     Austria
  archie.uqam.ca               132.208.250.10   Canada
  archie.funet.fi              128.214.6.102    Finland
  archie.univ-rennes1.fr       129.20.128.38    France
  archie.th-darmstadt.de       130.83.128.118   Germany
  archie.ac.il                 132.65.16.18     Israel
  archie.unipi.it              131.114.21.10    Italy
  archie.wide.ad.jp            133.4.3.6        Japan
  archie.hana.nm.kr            128.134.1.1      Korea
  archie.uninett.no            128.39.2.20      Norway
  archie.rediris.es            130.206.1.2      Spain
  archie.luth.se               130.240.12.30    Sweden
  archie.switch.ch             130.59.1.40      Switzerland
  archie.ncu.edu.tw            192.83.166.12    Taiwan
  archie.doc.ic.ac.uk          146.169.11.3     United Kingdom
  archie.hensa.ac.uk           129.12.21.25     United Kingdom
  archie.unl.edu               129.93.1.14      USA (NE)
  archie.internic.net          198.49.45.10     USA (NJ)
  archie.rutgers.edu           128.6.18.15      USA (NJ)
  archie.ans.net               147.225.1.10     USA (NY)
  archie.sura.net              128.167.254.179  USA (MD)
```

E-Mail: A Last Resort

It is possible to do both Archie and FTP by an awkward fix-up using only e-mail instead of either Unix commands or special software. The details are in Part VII because you only use this trick if you have a national on-line service that doesn't provide real Archie or FTP. Compared with using Anarchie or Fetch (explained later in this part), using e-mail is a ridiculous waste of time, but if it's your only way, you can at least make it work.

File Transfer Protocol (FTP)

Two years ago, the only way to do file transfers on the Internet was to use the standard Unix commands. Now, for all practical purposes, the Unix commands are a last resort.

After e-mail, file transfers are probably the second most important Internet function. Although some of the functions of traditional FTP are being absorbed into Gopher and Mosaic, FTP will be around for a few more years at least.

The Basics of FTP

Just as in standard Archie, the main snag in standard FTP is that you have to know where you're going and what you're trying to find. The assumption is that you got that information from your Archie searches, or you may simply have read about a cool file available at a particular server. (Write down that information!)

The following steps are for a command-based FTP:

1. Get to the system prompt on your Internet service provider (usually, >, $, or %).

```
About the Internet     FTP-File Transfer Protocol
Conference             Gopher
Databases (Files)      IRC-Internet Relay Chat
EMail                  Telnet
Forum (Messages)       Utilities (finger, traceroute, ping)
Guides (Books)         Usenet Newsgroups
Register/Cancel
Who's Here             Help
Workspace              Exit

Internet SIG>Enter your selection: ftp
Enter destination INTERNET address: coombs.anu.edu.au
Enter username (default: anonymous):


Enter password [chseiter@DELPHI.COM]: chseiter@delphi.com
|FTP| Open
```

2. Enter **ftp**.

The system asks you for a destination address, which you should have right in front of you, remember?

3. In most FTP transfers, your name is *anonymous* and your password is your Internet address. Enter this information.

A dazzling array of Unix remote-login information usually comes up.

The right side of the listing tells you where the files are; the lines in this listing that start with *d* are the equivalent of Macintosh folders.

```
220 coombs FTP server (Version wu-2.4(4) Wed Aug 24 20:19:53 EST 1994) ready.
331 Guest login ok, send your complete e-mail address as password.
230-Welcome to the Coombs Computing FTP service, it's Mon Nov  7 09:47:16 1994,
local time.
230-Please report any problems to -=- sean@coombs.anu.edu.au, thank you!
230-
230 Guest login ok, access restrictions apply.
FTP> dir

200 PORT command successful.
150 Opening ASCII mode data connection for /bin/ls.
total 36
drwxr-xr-x   8 root     root         1024 Dec 10  1993 .
drwxr-xr-x   8 root     root         1024 Dec 10  1993 ..
-rw-r--r--   1 papers   sys            59 May 23  1993 .message
d--x--x--x   2 root     root         1024 May 20  1993 bin
drwxr-xr-x   6 papers   root         1024 Oct 22 17:32 coombspapers
drwxr-xr-x  23 root     root         1024 Oct 18 12:26 pub

226 Transfer complete.
```

4. To get into one of these folders, you have to use the Unix command **cd**.

   In the figure, I typed **cd pub** to get to the directory (folder) called *pub* in the earlier listing.

```
FTP> cd pub

250-Hi! Excuse the mess, this archive is under deconstruction.
250-
250-Please read the file README
250-  it was last modified on Mon Jun 27 14:58:13 1994 - 133 days ago
250 CWD command successful.
FTP> dir

200 PORT command successful.
150 Opening ASCII mode data connection for /bin/ls.
226 Transfer complete.
total 100
drwxr-xr-x  23 root       root       1024 Oct 18 12:26 .
drwxr-xr-x   8 root       root       1024 Dec 10  1993 ..
-rw-r--r--   1 root       sys          59 May 23  1993 .message
drwxr-xr-x   4 papers     sys        1024 Oct 21 12:38 HISTLINK
drwxr-xr-x   3 181        sys        1024 Jul  4 12:25 SOCIOLOGY
drwxr-xr-x   4 244        413        1024 Oct 29 22:45 alt.sport.darts
drwxr-xr-x   6 477        666        1024 Sep 29 11:29 text
drwxr-xr-x   2 bryan      computing  1024 Oct 19 17:47 tmp
drwxr-xr-x   2 root       root       1024 Oct 17 14:01 unix
```

5. Use the command **dir** to get a listing of the files in this subdirectory (folder inside a folder).

6. Use the **cd** command again to get down to the basic file level.

   I typed **cd text**.

```
FTP> cd text

250 CWD command successful.
FTP> dir

200 PORT command successful.
150 Opening ASCII mode data connection for /bin/ls.
226 Transfer complete.
total 1736
drwxr-xr-x   6 477        666        1024 Sep 29 11:29 .
drwxr-xr-x  23 root       root       1024 Oct 18 12:26 ..
drwxr-xr-x   2 477        666          24 Jun 16  1992 IRCLogs
drwxr-xr-x   2 477        root       1024 Jun 24  1992 TCWF
-r--r--r--   1 477        666        6389 Sep 17  1992 crimes-act.txt
-rw-r--r--   2 root       sys      492528 Sep 29 11:29 zen-1.0.PS
-rw-r--r--   2 root       sys      190573 Sep 29 11:27 zen-1.0.PS.2
```

7. If you want a text file, type the command **ascii**. For a nontext file, you usually issue the command **binary**.

   In the figure, the file I want is crimes-act.txt.

8. Now type **get** and the filename to get the file and bring it back to your host computer.

The command **get crimes-act.txt mycrime.txt** means that the file will be renamed mycrime.txt on my home system.

```
FTP> ascii

FTP> get crimes-act.txt mycrime.txt

200 PORT command successful.
150 Opening ASCII mode data connection for crimes-act.txt (6389 bytes).
226 Transfer complete.
FTP> close

221 Goodbye.
FTP> exit

|FTP| Returning to host system....
```

9. Go through the host's procedure for downloading the file over your modem line.

What's happened is that the computer in Australia has sent, at a very high speed, the text file that I wanted to the Internet host computer. It's not yet on my Mac, which is why I need to download it. Details on downloading vary from system to system, but this screen is typical.

```
WS> (Please Select a Command) download

Download Method Menu:

XMODEM (128 byte blocks)     RT Buffer Capture
Kermit                       YB (YMODEM batch)
WXMODEM (Windowed XMODEM)    ZMODEM
YMODEM (1024 byte blocks)    Help
Buffer Capture               Exit

DOWNLOAD> (Xm,Kermit,WXm,Ym,Buff,RT,YB) zmodem
Name of file 1 for ZMODEM download to you ? mycrime.txt
(Batch contains 1 file:  6694 bytes = 12 YMODEM blocks, 54 XMODEM blocks)
  Press RETURN to begin downloading.
ZMODEM mode
Ok, receive! (1 file:  6694 bytes = 12 YMODEM blocks, 54 XMODEM blocks)

â*B00000000000000
FINAL STATUS = Transfer successful.
FINAL STATUS = 1 file successfully transferred.

Your file transfer method is now ZMODEM

WS> exit
```

E-Mail: A Last Resort

It is possible to do both Archie and FTP by an awkward fix-up using only e-mail instead of either Unix commands or special software. The details are in Part VII because you only use this trick if you have a national on-line service that doesn't provide real Archie or FTP. Compared with using Anarchie or Fetch, using e-mail is a ridiculous waste of time, but if it's your only way, it can at least be made to work.

Fetch: The Last Word in FTP

Even the Pipeline menu system is pretty clunky compared with the ultimate in file transfer programs: Dartmouth College's Fetch. I won't even bother to format this section as a formal series of steps, as you can just watch the figures and read the description of what may be called a click-and-enjoy interface. Like all Internet shareware, Fetch is available from standard archives, user groups, national on-line services, and Pipeline.

After you have made a SLIP connection (see Appendix A), double-click the Fetch icon.

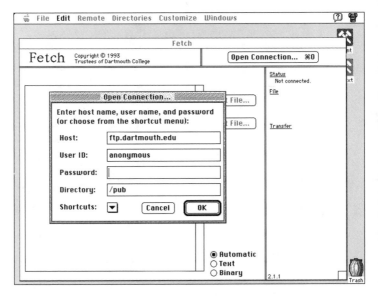

You'll see that Fetch is preloaded with the Internet address of the Dartmouth FTP site. Use this site only if it's later than 10 p.m. or so in New England — leave the computer to the students the rest of the time. As you can see in the following figure, the little scrolling list arrow under Shortcuts leads you to equivalent archives in different time zones, and you can add your own favorites to this list.

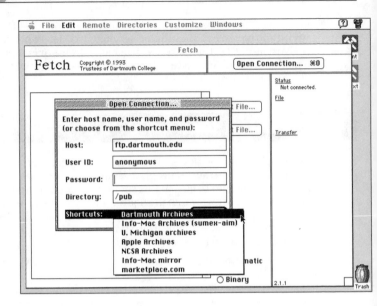

Click OK, and you get connected automatically to the FTP archive you have chosen. Notice that the little Fetch "doggie pointer" runs on-screen while information is being transferred.

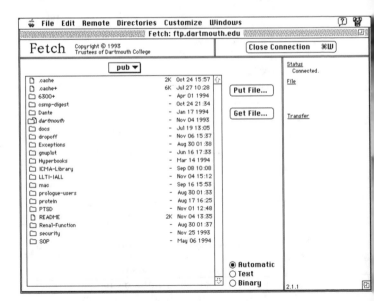

At this point, Fetch has converted the entire FTP file server to a giant Macintosh hard disk for your consideration. Click a folder to open it, and if you see something you like, click the Get File button. Not bad, eh?

But wait: there's more. Many Internet files are stored in the format .HQX (see the first figure following), which is a way of storing binary files as ASCII text so that they can be sent around as e-mail. (Don't worry about this issue too much; these file formats are going to be important mostly as nostalgic trivia when the Internet multimedia mail extensions are put into place everywhere.) Fetch automatically decodes these Unix-based formats when it transfers a selected file to your Mac (see the second figure following).

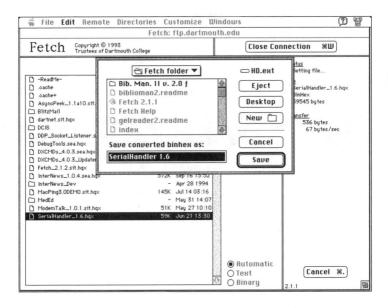

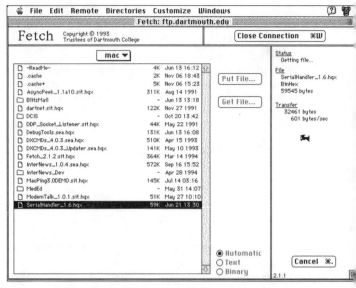

Menu-Based FTP

Menu-based FTPs offer better service than those that are command-based. America Online offers an FTP menu, and so does Pipeline, the service represented by the disk in *The Internet For Macs For Dummies Starter Kit.* A menu service gives you some choices even if you don't have the FTP list in front of you and recognizes that you want your Mac to be the destination for any transferred files.

Follow these simple steps to collect a file from a menu-based system such as Pipeline:

1. Look under "The Internet: Guides and Tools."

    FTP *is* just an Internet tool.

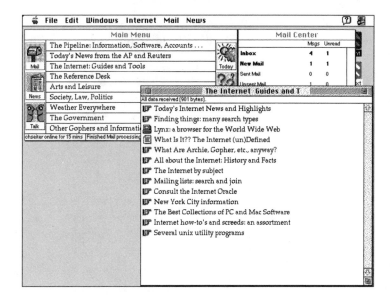

2. Under the last entry, "Several Unix utility programs," is Pipeline's own special FTP client. (The client is the program that runs on your computer, whereas the server runs on the Internet host.)

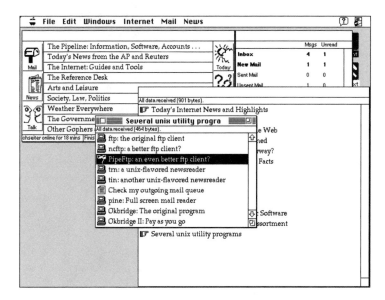

3. Enter the FTP site for the file transfer.

   This version of FTP handles the anonymous login, and it knows that you want the file transferred to your own computer without an intermediate step. You still have to know an FTP site for the transfer, but the rest of the details are handled automatically.

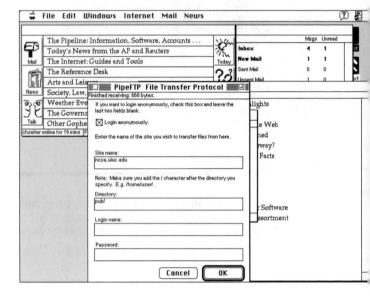

Part V

Gopher

Gopher also allows you to search for information on the Internet, and it is something of a latecomer to the Internet party, having been around in its current, highly refined forms for only a few years. That means two things:

- Gopher was designed with more built-in user convenience than traditional Unix-oriented systems.

- If you can do something in Gopher rather than the Archie/FTP combination, then do it in Gopher. It's just easier.

Once again, I give you a step-by-step tour of three different ways to use Gophers, ranging from terminal-type approaches to real Macintosh stuff. It's possible to envision an Internet world in which most low-level finding and fetching is done by Gopher and most fancier stuff is done with World Wide Web browsers (see Part VI). Actually, Parts II through VI are arranged in ascending order of both ease-of-use and gee-whiz.

I assume that you're here because you have access to some sort of Gopher service and are all fired up about downloading, so let's get started.

Good: Plain-Text Gopher

The most primitive version of Gopher is still a relatively sophisticated and user-friendly service compared to the telnet implementation of Archie. Most Gophers have similar structures, whether they are text-driven terminal-style programs or way-cool Macintosh programs. For reasons of symmetry, I'll start with the hard way.

1. Your Internet service provider (through a shell account or other dial-up service) should provide a menu with Gopher as a choice. Type **gopher** at the system prompt.

   A Gopher of some kind is now a part of Unix servers, bulletin boards, and all sorts of homemade information systems.

```
Internet SIG Menu:

About the Internet      FTP-File Transfer Protocol
Conference              Gopher
Databases (Files)       IRC-Internet Relay Chat
EMail                   Telnet
Forum (Messages)        Utilities (finger, traceroute, ping)
Guides (Books)          Usenet Newsgroups
Register/Cancel
Who's Here              Help
Workspace               Exit

Internet SIG>Enter your selection: gopher
```

2. Pick something from the Gopher menu by double-clicking it.

Although there's some variation, the following list is pretty standard. The Gopher menu offers specialized areas (law, medicine), other search methods (including WWW), and usually a choice for All The World's Gophers. In this case, I picked All The World because it's 4:30 a.m. in Australia.

```
Internet SIG Gopher
Page 1 of 1

1    PERSONAL FAVORITES                                        Menu
2    "ABOUT DELPHI'S GOPHER SERVICE"                           Text
3    *** FAQ: FREQUENTLY ASKED QUESTIONS *** (REVISED 11/4)    Menu
4    ALL THE WORLD'S GOPHERS                                   Menu
5    BUSINESS AND ECONOMICS                                    Menu
6    COMPUTERS                                                 Menu
7    FREE-NETS AND COMMUNITY ACCESS                            Menu
8    FTP: DOWNLOADABLE PROGRAMS, IMAGES, SOUNDS                Menu
9    GAMES AND MUDS, MUSHES, MUSES, AND MOOS                   Menu
10   GOVERNMENT AND POLITICS                                   Menu
11   HEALTH AND MEDICINE                                       Menu
12   INTERNET INFORMATION                                      Menu
13   LAW                                                       Menu
14   LIBRARIES AND RESEARCH GUIDES                             Menu
15   SCHOOLHOUSE (K-12)                                        Menu
16   SEARCH UTILITIES                                          Menu
17   SUBJECT MATTER MENUS                                      Menu
18   THE GRAB BAG (WITH WHAT'S NEW 10/20)                      Menu
19   WORLD WIDE WEB                                            Menu
```

The world, of course, is a fairly big place (at least, it's the biggest we've got right now). The All The World command gets you a view of the world in which Minnesota is especially prominent because the Gopher originated there.

```
ALL THE WORLD'S GOPHERS
Page 1 of 2

1    Connect to any gopher (Type a gopher address)    Search
2    Search for Gophers by Partial Name or Address    Search
3    Search for Gophers by Partial Name or Address    Search
4    DELPHI Gophers                                   Menu
5         ****SELECTED SPECIAL INTEREST GOPHERS****   Text
6    Carnegie Mellon U English Server                 Menu
7    Gopher Jewels                                    Menu
8    Library of Congress MARVEL Gopher                Menu
9    RiceInfo, Rice U                                 Menu
10   University of North Carolina (SunSite)           Menu
11   U of Minnesota (the mother of all gophers)       Menu
12   Mother gopher (UMinn) by telnet                  Telnet
13   Washington & Lee U                               Menu
14   WHAT'S NEW?: New Gophers List (updated daily)    Menu
15        ****GOPHERS BY GEOGRAPHICAL LOCATION****    Text
16   USA Gophers                                      Menu
17   United Nations Gopher                            Menu
18   International Organizations                      Menu
19   Africa                                           Menu
```

3. Select a choice from the list of available Gophers.

My friends the Australians are under Pacific in this list (it's on the second page of choices). Because of my morbid interest in crime, I select choice 15 in this set (this selection takes me to the same place as some examples in Part V).

```
Pacific
Page 1 of 3

1    AARNET                                                         Menu
2    AgResearch Wallaceville, Upper Hutt, New Zealand               Menu
3    Austin Hospital, Melbourne, Australia                          Menu
4    Australian Defence Force Academy (Canberra, Australia)         Menu
5    Australian Environmental Resources Information Network (ERIN    Menu
6    Australian Graduate School of Management, University of New     Menu
7    Australian National Botanic Gardens                            Menu
8    Australian National University                                 Menu
9    BioInformatics gopher at ANU                                   Menu
10   Cairo Gopher                                                   Menu
11   Centre for Design at RMIT (Royal Melbourne Institute of Tech    Menu
12   Centre for University Teaching & Learning - University of So    Menu
13   Charles Sturt University                                       Menu
14   Computer Systems Engineering, Royal Melbourne Institute of T    Menu
15   Coombsquest - ANU Soc.Sci & Humanities Inf.Facility            Menu
16   Curtin University of Technology, Western Australia              Menu
17   Flinders University                                            Menu
18   Griffith University                                            Menu
19   ILANET and State Library of NSW Gopher                         Menu
```

4. Select something from the next menu.

Choice 7 in the next menu takes you back to the old file on crime under the COOMBSPAPERS archive.

```
COOMBSPAPERS - ANU Soc.Sci.Research Data Bank - FTP Archives
Page 1 of 1

1    Search the "ANU-Coombspapers-Index" database                  Search
2    About ANU Social Sciences Information Services (Coombspapers   Text
3    Meta-INDEX to the Coombsapers collection (Coombspapers,ANU)    Text
4    Detailed INDEX files of the Coombspapers archive (ANU)         Menu
5    Coombsarchives collection (Coombspapers,ANU)                   Menu
6    Otherarchives collection (Coombspapers,ANU)                    Menu
7    COOMBSPAPERS - ANU Soc.Sci.Research Data Bank - FTP Mirrors    Menu

Enter Item Number, SAVE, ?, or BACK: 3

File information from FTP directory:

-rw-r-----  1 papers   root      16742 Nov  2 08:02
/coombspapers/COOMBSPAPERS-META-INDEX

Press ENTER to display, D to Download, C to Cancel:
Retrieving text via FTP - press Control-C at any time to cancel
```

Notice that, at the end of this menu, you can display text files
directly or simply choose D for download. Again, download
means that you have taken the file from Australia to your Internet
host and will have to download it yet again to your own Mac. But
this whole exercise is far simpler that an Archie/FTP exercise.
That's actually the point of software development: to make things
so simple that even a ...*For Dummies* book is overkill (don't worry,
it will never happen!).

In a text menu-driven system, a key disadvantage is that you have
to step all the way back through the menus, one choice at a time,
to return to your starting point. That's not a critical drawback,
however, because text-based systems are so well adapted to
modem transmission (it takes less than a second to fill a screen
with a 9600 bps modem) that the lag isn't too annoying.

Notice that you don't have to know anything about changing
directories in a Unix-based system, and you have the option of
downloading directly as soon as you find the file or files you want.
That's why I expect Gopher largely to replace the older utilities in
everyday practice. Actually, applications like Fetch and
TurboGopher (discussed later in this part) are really starting to
merge in functionality.

Better: Pipeline's Gopher

I should state my prejudice explicitly: "better," in reference to
software, means that I can slap an Empty Tank = No Brainer icon
on a description. Hey, I've been working for *Macworld* for ten
years, and after reviewing several hundred programs, I've
developed an affection for software that you can learn in ten
minutes.

Having said that, I will now trace the steps in finding material in
Pipeline's Gopher. (The steps are nearly the same in America
Online.)

1. Find the Gopher service.

   This step should be pretty easy — the service is just a topic
   listed as Other Gophers and Information Servers.

   Note the following figure, in which this advanced graphical
   environment also has an All The World's Gophers option.

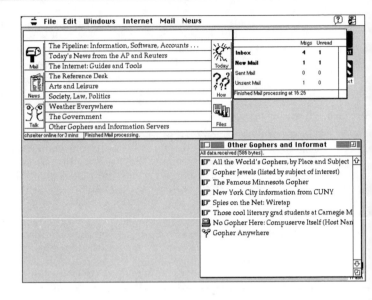

2. Choose the All option to see the Gophers in a standard Macintosh scrolling list.

   At this point, I could simply produce a name for a site in Australia from my own list, but there's a choice for Australia already on the list.

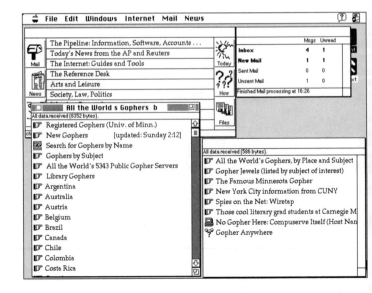

Well, mates, OZ is a fair-dinkum wonderland of coral reefs, exotic fauna, and Internet sites. In the following figure, you see a major advantage of a real graphical menu system for Gopher — you can click right to Minnesota from this screen without backing out of three or four menus.

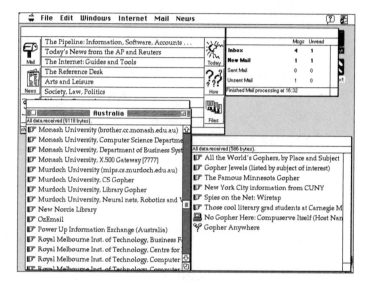

I click the Australian National University to get the display in the next figure. At this point, you need to understand a bit about the icon system in the menus — if there's a little hand pointer, you go down another level in the menus if you select it. On the other hand, the icons that look like TeachText documents are plain text. Only occasionally at most of these more remote Gopher archives do you find actual programs. Very often, they are repositories of scholarly reports and conference proceedings.

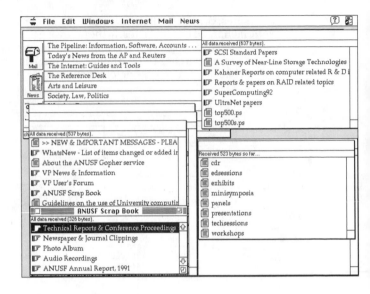

3. Click a text document to open it.

   In this type of menu, it appears in its own window. You can copy and paste the text into a Macintosh word processor, or you can save the whole window as text. (In Pipeline, there's a command under the File menu.)

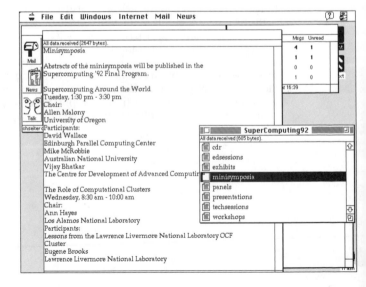

This particular example, by the way, is fairly representative of what you find when you drill down a Gopher menu. There's lots of computer science and academic information, but not much in the way of punk-music clips, business directories, or cultural events. Most of that material has migrated to the World Wide Web, while Gophers are still a backbone of information exchange in the universities of the world.

Best: TurboGopher

 It takes a bit of work to set up a SLIP account (Appendix A), but once you have it, you can use TurboGopher, the University of Minnesota's own pride and joy. It's universally distributed at the same places as all other Internet public-domain and shareware programs.

Here's how you use TurboGopher:

 1. After making a SLIP connection (I recommend leaving the InterSLIP window open so you can make sure that your connection has not dropped back to Idle), just double-click the TurboGopher icon.

   It automatically connects itself to the University of Minnesota as a default.

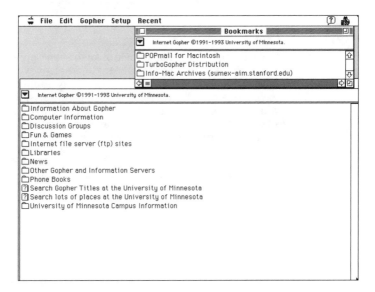

2. Click the Other Gophers folder.

   You see a set of folders remarkably similar to those you have seen in the less-sophisticated Gopher examples. That's because the people in Minnesota pretty much define the idea of a "good" Gopher, and everyone else imitates them.

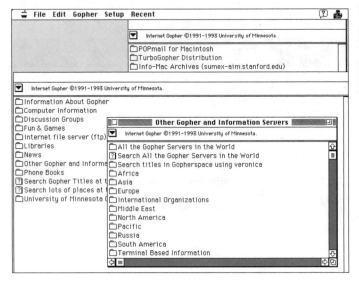

3. Click the Pacific folder.

   You have the old familiar choice of Australian Gopher sites. You can just as well pick European Gophers, or even American Gophers. The reality is that many Gopher servers have the same collection of Mac files — the decision about which Gopher to choose is based on access. In this mode, sites appear as folders instead of as numbered menu choices, but the information content is the same.

Basically, you can click your way around the globe. TurboGopher has converted all the computers at all the Gopher sites on the planet into extended versions of your own hard drive.

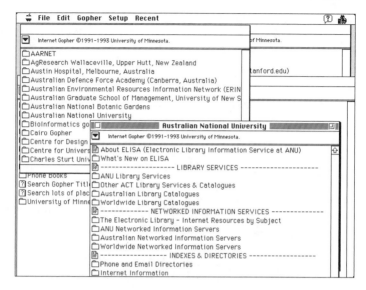

Other TurboGopher services

TurboGopher, as a service that "rides on top of" other information services, offers you several search options — one of the
reasons that you can expect simpler utilities to become less
popular over the years.

First, TurboGopher *incorporates* other search types. If you need to
find FTP sites or perform Archie searches, you can do them from
within TurboGopher.

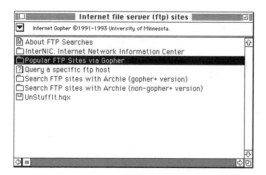

Second, you can immediately pop back to any point in your
search chain. The Recent menu contains all the information about
this particular session of TurboGopher, so you can simply choose
this menu item and retrace your steps or head back to square one.

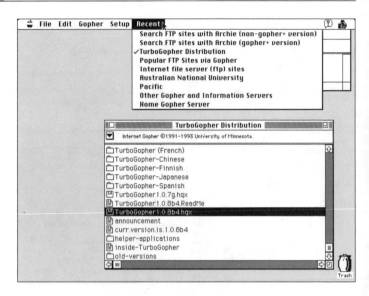

Finally, notice that this site is, of course, the home of new, updated, feature-rich, and faster versions of TurboGopher. Although the current version in English is available nearly everywhere, the FTP site boombox.micro.umn.edu has foreign versions and lots of other information about optimal Gopher use.

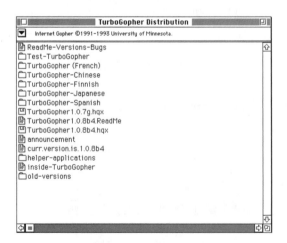

Unlike the problems you are likely to find at Archie servers (see Part IV), TurboGopher usually has no problem checking in to its home site. The University of Minnesota has decided to rise nobly to the occasion and devote extra resources to supporting its offspring. The Configuration dialog box on the current version of TurboGopher shows that a backup system has been installed to make sure that you can get through to the site, unless, of course, you insist on trying it at 1:30 p.m. on Wednesday. (Don't!)

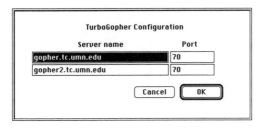

Part VI

The WWW and Mosaic

What's the World Wide Web?

You already know about *hypertext* (a set of text files in which individual words link one file to the next) if you've done anything with HyperCard. Click an underlined or bold term in a hypertext document, and you are transported to another document page. The biggest hypertext project on the planet, a direct Internet result of earlier efforts in information processing, is the World Wide Web, which is simply an Internet service consisting of hypertext-linked documents. The difference between the WWW and a Mac HyperCard stack is simple but impressive — the hyperlink (hypertext link) usually takes you to information *on another computer.*

The WWW uses *hypertext markup language* (HTML) — the native dialect of the World Wide Web. HTML is simply a set of formatting directives that define the hypertext links — the links that take you to a new Web page when you click an underlined keyword in another page. Just as there's an FTP (file transfer protocol) and a SLIP (serial line interface protocol), there's an HTTP, for *hypertext transport protocol,* that serves as the connection protocol for World Wide Web.

When you fire up special-purpose software for browsing the Web, you open a URL (for *Uniform Resource Locator*), give it a resource such as http://www.commerce.net/, and your browser connects you to a world of HTML pages. You can think of these HTTP locations as the e-mail addresses of the Web. They typically take you to a home page, which is just a WWW document containing links to other pages.

This stuff sounds a bit dry and in fact, text-based WWW was not really setting the world on fire. But this system has two big advantages built in, just waiting to be exploited:

- **The Web knows where you're going.** The links contain information for automatically telnetting to other WWW sites. In the old style of "surfing the Internet," you needed to know all your destinations in advance. This method was more like skateboarding a construction site than surfing — unless you were good at jumping and knew the terrain, you wouldn't get far. Once you're on a WWW site, by contrast, all you do is click links.

- **The Web's got pictures.** Graphics are, of course, cool in general, but if you want people to order garden equipment over the Internet, graphics are essential. A big part of the rush to expand the WWW in the mid-1990s was the drive to put business on the Internet, with catalogs, order forms, annual reports, and even employment offers. All these documents work better with a text/graphics mix than with text alone.

Mosaic Takes Over

Mosaic is a graphic Web browser that enables you to easily find stuff on the Internet. At one point, the World Wide Web (WWW)/ Mosaic situation looked like a chicken-and-egg problem — there really wasn't much material on the Web, so there wasn't much demand for Web browsers. But the original version of Mosaic created at NCSA (National Center for Supercomputing Applications, in Urbana, Illinois) was just so much fun to use that more than a million people downloaded it, creating a big window on the Web. All sorts of universities, businesses, and other organizations, therefore, began furiously filling the Web with material.

When you activate a SLIP connection (see Appendix A) and double-click the Mosaic icon, you connect automatically to the NCSA Home Page. If you don't have Mosaic yet, you can download the current version from a national on-line service (America Online, CompuServe, and others) or fetch it directly by anonymous FTP to `ftp:pub.ncsa.uiuc.edu`.

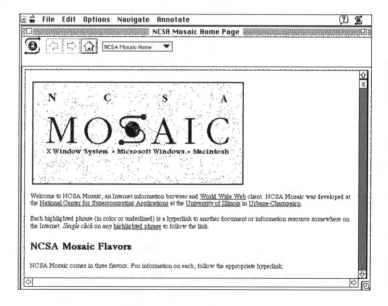

You should notice a few key points about this page, especially because all other graphical Web browsers are nearly trivial variations on this one. First, near the top are little arrows pointing to the left and right — you can click these to go backward or

forward in your path. Another way to navigate is with the
scrolling list (it says NCSA Home Page in this picture), which
keeps track of all the places you have visited. Because in a busy
half-hour you may visit four or five places, the ability to jump
back six places in the list is often quite helpful. Of course, you can
also get back to the Home Page at any time by clicking the little
house icon at the top of the page.

When Mosaic was first developed, all its users were connected to
Cray computers over high-speed fiber optic links. Because users
were working with a system that could deliver megabits/sec, they
could click any highlighted phrase and follow the link without
worrying about time considerations. If you're using Mosaic over a
9600-bps modem-based SLIP connection, however, some of these
links can blow up into forty-minute downloads. Also, the software
isn't particularly graceful about being interrupted. Be prepared to
turn your modem off if you see messages like `Transferring
8128 bytes out of 4357219 bytes` at the top of the screen
in a Web browser such as Mosaic.

Mosaic step-by-step?

Usually in a *...For Dummies Quick Reference,* you find lots of little
numbered lists for step-by-step use of a particular piece of
software. Here are the steps for Mosaic:

1. Click any highlighted word or phrase that sounds interesting to you.

2. Repeat Step 1.

I know this sounds silly, but that's all you have to do! Mosaic is
enormously popular because you can use it right away — no one
has even had the audacity to propose a training course, and a
whole book about Mosaic would be a strange creature indeed. In
this part, I show you some of the scope of the resources available
through Mosaic on WWW. I don't give you many steps because
there aren't any. Using Mosaic is more like clicking through TV
channels with a remote control than, say, flowing text around an
irregular graphic in Microsoft Word.

Where do you go from here? I recommend scrolling down this
page to the What's New section because the WWW has more
genuinely new stuff every week than, oh, all the national TV
networks have produced since the day you were born.

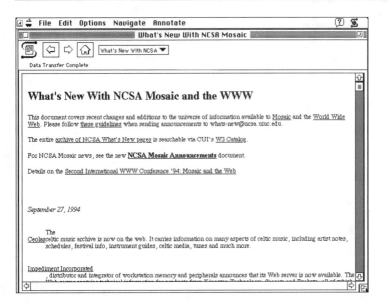

Using Mosaic to Roam Around on the Web

When you use the arrows or click the home icon, you will be relieved to find that Mosaic has *cached,* or stored, enough material to show you something right away. Because some Web documents are not just long but also full of graphics, getting results can obviously take a long time, even at 14.4 Kps. Rather than just scrolling through new topics (although doing so can entertain you for days), you may want to check the whole W3 catalog (*W3* is equivalent to WWW). This catalog, which will have more than 10,000 entries by the time you get to it, is typical of the hefty files lumbering around the Web — the *recent changes* link alone is a 250K download (as shown on the first figure on the next page).

One of the first things you'll find after dipping into this W3 catalog is that You Are Not Alone. Living in North America, a giant land mass with thousands of miles of cold salt water at either side, it's easy to forget the reality of the rest of the planet. On the WWW, the rest of the planet jumps right down your modem wire and splashes onto your screen. Here you see the language menu of Deutsche Welle, roughly the German equivalent of the BBC. Most services looking for an international audience will have to provide language menus just like that shown in the second figure on the next page.

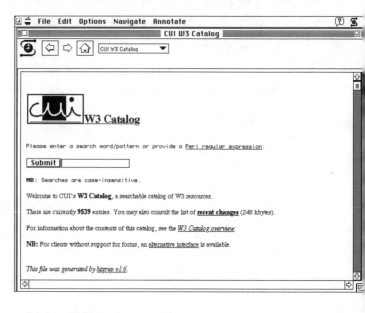

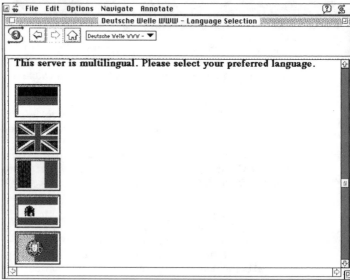

The Internet as Entertainment

I suspect, although I cannot prove, that most readers of this book are not fired up about Mosaic solely because it will give them access to Portuguese language math papers from the University of Coimbra (which it does).

Maybe you had something a little lighter in mind. How about the official Web site for the world's most profitable elderly rock collective, which you can find right on the What's New page at NCSA? There they are, ladiesandgentlementheRollingStones, costing you about five extra minutes on-line to download all those little tongues and other icons before you get to the merchandise for sale.

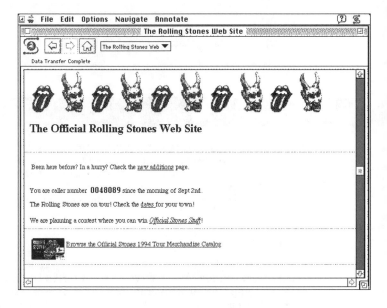

A site that's more important for Mac users of the WWW is the Well Connected Mac, which has connections to other Web sites, to vendors, and to mailing lists and also makes a beginning attempt at doing e-mail through the Web. Find this site in the NCSA What's New section (until March 1995 or so) or send e-mail to elharo@shock.njit.edu for more information.

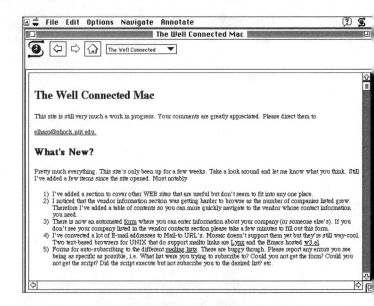

Other Web Browsers

As fine a product as Mosaic is, there are perfectly good alternatives. Mosaic was the first graphic Web browser, and its developers deserve a world of credit, but it's not going to be the final word on the WWW. Now that programmers have had a good look at Mosaic, you can expect faster, smaller alternatives to pop up everywhere.

MacWeb

MacWeb, available from `ftp.galaxy.einet.net` and from almost every national on-line service's software library, is fast, efficient, compact, and has one impressive advantage: It starts up from a home page at `galaxy.einet.net` that never seems to be crowded (see the next figure).

One key feature of MacWeb is that it shows graphics icons where they're present but doesn't download the graphics unless instructed. On the Rolling Stones page, for example, you see all the tongues only if you insist on opening the graphics files. As a result, you get files about three times faster with MacWeb than with Mosaic. A page of text takes about 2K of file space, and a page of 8-bit color takes several hundred K, so there's a pretty

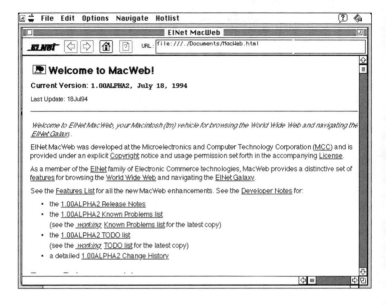

compelling logic to keeping graphics files buttoned up until you decide that you want them. There's a big difference in display time between the next two WWW Virtual Library figures.

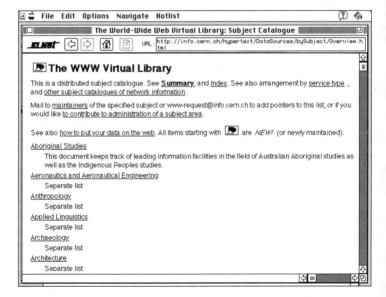

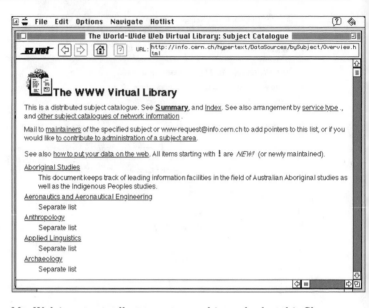

MacWeb is not actually averse to graphics — look at this Chance database home page, showing merry mathematical revelers trying to beat the odds in its title bar. You owe it to yourself to peruse Chance. Note the following URL tag for Chance:

```
http://www.geom.umn.edu/docs/snell/chance/welcome.html/
```

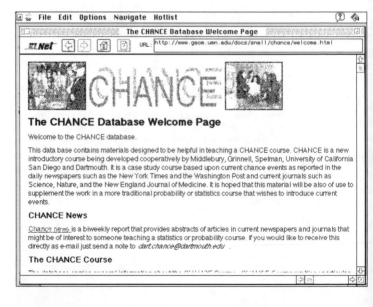

If you ever feel the need to interpret for yourself all these strange studies that appear in newspapers claiming that toasted almonds cure glaucoma or that second-hand smoke rots your tires, a weekly perusal of Chance is a good place to start.

Spyglass, Inc. (or What's on the Web horizon)

Other organizations have also produced Web browsers: Spyglass, Inc. has an official license to make OEM versions of Mosaic, for example. But what you'll see in 1995 and beyond is a profusion of Web browsers. Some of them will be custom programs for national on-line services, some will be commercial software, and some will be shareware. The real heavy lifting in the Web project came in defining Web structure and the mark-up language. Writing a browser is nowhere near as grand a challenge as defining the Web in the first place.

You may find that you're already working for a company with a site license for a special version of Mosaic from Spyglass, Inc. There aren't many operational feature differences between the version of Mosaic I'm describing here and the Spyglass Enhanced Mosaic edition. Spyglass's product is more compact, is faster, has better Help, and has a snappy Power Mac version. Another big difference is that you'll be using it on a network at work, so all the remarks about slow downloads don't apply.

Doing Business on the Web

If you think that the Stones want to sell you things on the Web, wait until you hear from General Motors. To sell things on-line, you need to be able to show people pictures. That's why Mosaic, in several variations, has been the basis of most Internet business action.

The easiest way to follow developments is to fire up Mosaic, head to the What's New section of the NCSA Mosaic home page on the WWW, and scroll down through the list of selections. You'll find non-profits such as the Library of Congress and universities, but you will also see platoons of businesses, typically signed up with one business network or other.

The Internet Business Center, for example, provides not only a way to sell your own services but also access to papers on marketing and commercial Internet statistics.

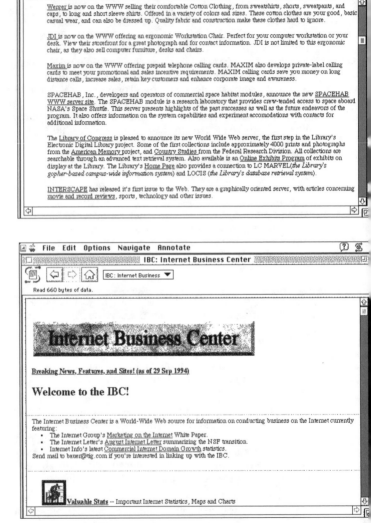

Finding stuff to buy

Another connection is the Internet Shopping Network (800-677-7467), which can provide you with a range of services. The

ISN has taken into account some of the problems of the full-graphics approach to the WWW — unless you have a connection that runs at 56 Kps or better, in which case you need, as an alternative, lots of patience.

One of the areas you may want to visit is the Macintosh software area on the Internet Shopping Network. Basically, every piece of Macintosh software is there, waiting only for your order, and it's there at a discount. This is probably one of the marketing areas on the Internet that will actually work because of the following reasons:

- **Customers already know the products.** You can read a review of Microsoft Excel 5, and if you're using Version 4.1, you can decide whether you want to upgrade. The vendor doesn't have a big selling job to do.

- **They're *computer* products.** If you find yourself looking at a Mosaic screen for the Internet Shopping Network, you're in the first few percent of Internet pioneers and are likely the kind of person who buys upgrades.

- **Software purchasing is pretty straightforward.** There are no different sizes or colors. And an Internet shopping service can give you the same level of service as a paper catalog, only faster.

By the way, it's not just computer stuff out there on the Net. Specialized organizations are putting multipart catalogs and giant webs of directories together to service whole industries. You can expect to see every industry and subindustry with its own WWW information service by mid-1995. This will be possible partly because the organizations driving commercialization are so helpful and ambitious and partly because developing HTML documents gets to be pretty easy once you have a modicum of practice. Just keep logging on to the home pages for NCSA and Galaxy and scroll down to check what's new.

Officially, you can get anywhere on the Web just by clicking. In practice, if you keep a little notebook of URL HTTP addresses, you can get there much faster. Make a note of how many times you open a particular URL, and if you use one more than a few times a week, add it to the URL list, as part of the Hot List under the Mosaic annotate menu or under the File menu of other browsers.

Setting up shop

If you have a modest array of products to sell, you may want to look at the WWW mall operated by Internet ShopKeeper.

The first such services were designed for big organizations like Pacific Bell and Amdahl Computers, but Internet ShopKeeper is pretty close to an ideal service for small businesses. One reason it's ideal is that the rates are survivably low. Instead of a $2,000 setup fee and a $500-per-month on-line charge, the setup fee is $5 and the rates are probably less than your phone bill.

This remark about Internet ShopKeeper is meant to give you a starting point for discussions at the office with some current information. If you're serious about WWW business opportunities, your best bet is to follow network news in *Macworld* every month. The scene changes every few *weeks* as new vendors try to stake out claims in the great Internet Gold Rush of 1994.

Part VII

The Internet and On-Line Services

In this chapter, I discuss using the Internet facilities of the main national on-line services: America Online, CompuServe, Prodigy, Delphi, and GEnie. Although I'm an Apple fan, a devoted Mac user, and an eWorld beta tester, I don't think that eWorld will ever be a first choice for Internet access, despite its great interface.

The on-line business story is that services like Prodigy were constructed at mind-numbing expense, signed up millions of users, and never made enough money to make their investors happy. Along came the Internet, an uncensored network amalgam of news, e-mail, serious computer stuff, and sheer silliness, and everyone found it more interesting than the carefully prepared on-line services. Right now, providing access to the Internet is the best hope of lighting a new commercial spark that most of these services have.

These services are not all created equal. I'll give you some step-by-step instructions for using the Internet on each service, but I'll also point out deficiencies where they exist.

This part, you may notice, is longer than most other parts of the book. That's because, one way or another, Internet access through on-line services is destined to replace do-it-yourself Internet for the vast majority of users over the next few years. *You* pay these guys, and then *they* make it easy.

America Online

For combining an easy-to-use interface with a good assortment of real-Internet services, AOL is the leader of the pack.

What you get

In late 1994, America Online included the following:

- Internet e-mail, inbound and outbound
- USENET newsgroups
- A Gopher service and access to other remote Gophers
- Wide-Area Information Servers (WAIS)
- File Transfer Protocol (FTP) service

Before January 1995, AOL should introduce a graphical WWW browser. It may also provide access to Archie servers, but this capability may not develop because you can use Gopher to find the same file information.

Using AOL for the Internet

TIP

When you log onto AOL, you can go directly to the Macintosh Software Center. The reason I point this out is that 98 percent of the files that are actually interesting in the big archives at Stanford, Michigan, and elsewhere — archives that are now jammed with requests around the clock — are available directly on AOL. So look in this forum first and help keep the Net from clogging up solid with people downloading the same game files.

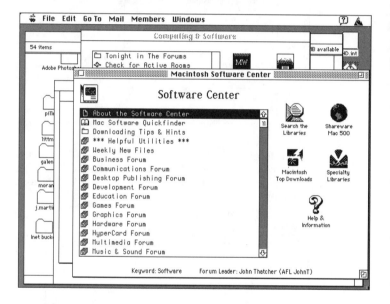

Getting there

From the main AOL screen (the one you see when you sign on), pull down the Go To menu, pick Keyword from the choices, and type **internet** in the dialog box. Then the screen should change to the glorious vista you see on the next page.

The list at the left contains an amazing amount of material. For example, it contains the full text, arranged in searchable form, of Brendan Kehoe's admirable *Zen and the Art of the Internet*. If you don't like my explanations, you can try one of his, although his book is mostly a guide to old-style Unix telecommunications. When you double-click About the Internet Center, you get AOL's own explanation of its services.

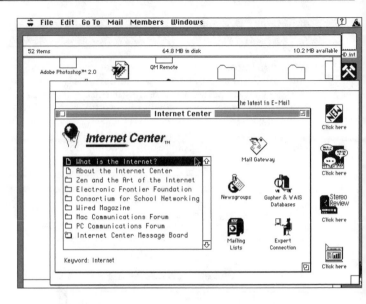

On the Internet Center Message Board, you can see announcements of new services. There you'll also see AOL management being mercilessly slagged by impatient users waiting for a Web Browser.

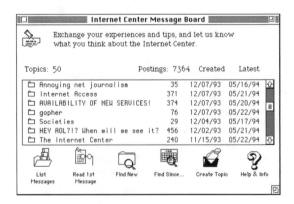

E-Mail

Type the Keyword **internet** again and click the Mail Gateway icon to get this screen:

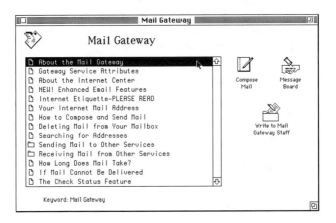

Here's what to do to send a message for the first time:

1. Read the message on Internet etiquette.

   Etiquette in this sense means being careful about addressing messages so that they don't clog up the wrong e-mail mailboxes.

2. Read the document called Your Internet Mail Address.

   Sending and receiving mail is handled automatically by AOL, and you can put your new Internet address (you@aol.com) on your business cards.

3. Click the Compose Mail icon.

   You get a window with a simple Macintosh word processor.

4. Simply cut and paste text into the message area.

   Similarly, you can cut sections of messages you receive and paste them into standard documents in other applications.

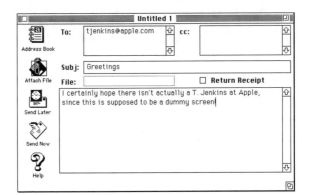

5. In the To: box at the top of the form, you list an Internet address the same way you list an AOL internal address (in AOL lingo, a screen name).

Newsgroups

Connecting to USENET newsgroups is very straightforward in AOL. Follow these steps:

1. Click the Newsgroups icon in the main Internet screen.

2. To add newsgroups to the AOL default list, you can either use the Search option (you enter topics) or use Expert Add if you know the name of the newsgroup.

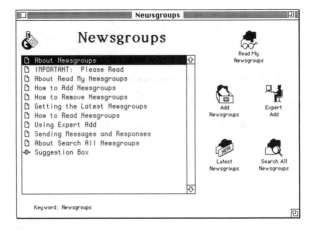

Refer to Appendix C of this Quick Reference for a long list of newsgroup names. AOL does not volunteer the names of most adult-content groups, but you can add them with Expert Add. Having said that, let me implore you not to bother trying to collect low-resolution erotic pictures from AOL or other Internet sources. If you want this stuff, print media still has a great technological advantage.

Mailing lists

Mailing lists are just collections of Internet e-mail addresses. The mailing list system evolved mainly as a way for researchers at widely separated institutions to keep in touch. The biggest set of mailing lists, in fact, evolved separately from the Internet on BITNET, although there's considerable crossover.

On AOL, you can sign up for any of these discussion groups just by adding your name to the list, and you can quit a group just as easily. Click the mailing list icon in the first Internet Center screen, and you get the following screen:

 Note these mailing list precautions:

- Once you join a list, you should probably monitor it every day for the first few days to get an idea of the traffic volume. If you sign up for lots of active lists, you'll find that your AOL mailbox limit (550 messages) can be reached quite rapidly.

- You should also read the messages for a week or so to determine whether you really have a contribution to make to the other list members. Think about whether you'll be wasting your own time and someone else's time getting involved in an endless series of messages.

Gopher and WAIS

AOL evaluated dozens of Gopher and WAIS sites for reliability and then wrote an interface in which you, the end user, can't always tell whether you're getting information from a Gopher site or a WAIS server. You get the information, but you don't get the search path or the Internet details.

Here's how to find information on nearly any topic:

1. Double-click the Gopher icon at the main Internet Center screen.

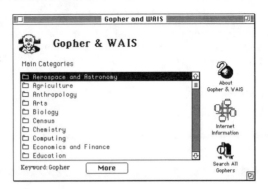

At present, AOL has loaded a large array of topics into what appears to be its own site, so searches are fast and don't usually connect you to other computers.

2. Click the Search All Gophers icon to perform a Veronica search over all available Gophers and to find specific subjects.

FTP

AOL still hasn't decided how to implement full telnet (it's probably more a question of billing than anything else), but the service imple-mented FTP in October 1994. This is how you perform an FTP file transfer:

1. To get FTP service, find FTP in the Internet Center window (keyword: Internet).

Doing so gets you the FTP window with options that include an explanation of the service.

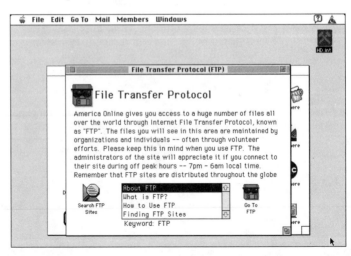

2. To see a set of the most likely FTP archives for finding popular files, pick the Go To FTP option.

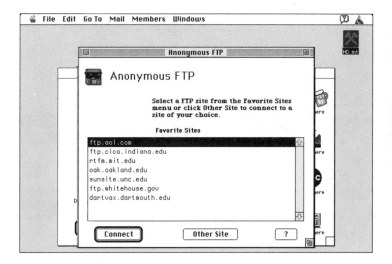

How it rates

If you're an Internet beginner and a Mac user besides, AOL Internet is the right place to start. It would be easy to spend several months just exploring AOL's regular services and the Internet areas. AOL has done a not-perfect, but very good, job of making the Internet accessible to Mac users just starting out in communications. And it's getting better. As I review the other national on-line systems in the next few sections, you'll see why I recommend AOL to friends.

CompuServe

CompuServe has advantages and disadvantages. For example, its collection of files that you may want to download is quite impressive. It should be impressive because CompuServe has been collecting files since the dawn of time, at least in computer terms. A big disadvantage is that lots of things on CompuServe are done in a particular way because that's the way they have always been done. The design choices were made back in the days of slow computers and even slower networks and don't represent the state-of-the-art in comparison to newer services such as America Online.

What you get

In late 1994, CompuServe provided the following:

- Internet e-mail
- By-mail FTP and Archie
- Internet information services
- Newsgroups

Using CompuServe for the Internet

In traditional CompuServe, you did most of your navigating by picking numbers. The system presented you with a numbered menu, and you responded with the number of your choice. These days, most CompuServe access is bundled with CompuServe Information Manager (CIM), part of the starter kit that you buy in computer stores.

Information services

If you choose Go from the Services menu and type **inetforum**, you get the following encouraging screen:

File Edit Services Messages Libraries Conference Special					

Library Files

View Topics   Info   **Abstract**   Mark   View   Retrieve   Delete

Messages since Sat, Jun   Browsing "FTP & File Transfer [6] "

Section	Filename	Title	Submitted	Size	Accesses
General Information	MACFTP.TXT	Mac-FTP-list Version 3.8.6	6/1/94	39.5K	158
Getting Started [2]	WNCODE.ZIP	Windows UUEncode & Decode	5/1/94	55.5K	828
Internet Access [3]	CD.TXT	INTERNET VIRUS	5/1/94	2179	1088
Directory Services [	WNCOD2.ZIP	Wincode V2.3	4/26/94	251.5K	546
Electronic Mail [5]	GZIPLH.EXE	gzip 1.1 for .z & .gz & .Z files. UNCO...	4/9/94	48.5K	622
FTP & File Transfer	WEIRDI.ZIP	Weird Sites on the Internet	3/20/94	43K	1809
Newsgroups/Usenet [	COMPRS.ZIP	File Compression FAQ	3/2/94	72K	498
Mailing Lists [8]	AUDIOF.ZIP	Audio File Formats FAQ	3/2/94	37K	259
Gopher / WAIS / WW	NCFTP.DOC	Info on ncftp, an alternative to ftp	2/28/94	38K	218
International [10]	FTPLOC.ZIP	Anonymous FTP Site Listing	2/22/94	99.5K	3005
Resources-Academic	FTPFAQ.ZIP	Anonymous FTP FAQ	2/22/94	10K	1685
Resources-Business	FTPDOS.ZIP	Recommended MS-DOS shareware/fr...	2/22/94	26K	2601
Resources-Communi	FTPNET.ZIP	Anonymous ftp from the Internet via ...	2/21/94	101.5K	2837
Resources-Govt. [14	FTPHOW.TXT	How to use anonymous FTP (Internet ...	2/18/94	26.5K	2923
Resources-Technical					
Resources-Personal					
Resources-Mac [17]					

This screen shows CompuServe's amazing collection of resources for finding out about the Internet. It does not, however, connect you to very many services. It's got libraries with the programs you need for Internet connection, but, ironically, you can't use the programs here.

Late in 1995, CompuServe Information Services decided to develop a special Internet service, but that service is for businesses rather than individuals. CompuServe has long been a vendor of special information services, and, in fairness, I should point out that it offers information that you can't find, or can't find in a convenient form, on the Internet itself. Its Drug Reference database (use the Go command to *drug reference*) is the equivalent of the *Physician's Desk Reference* and is better organized than analogous public-domain software.

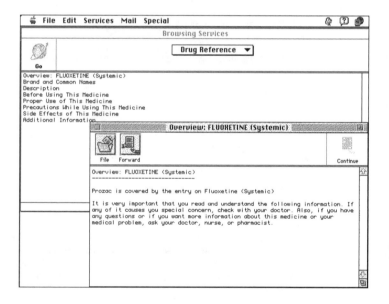

E-Mail

CompuServe e-mail is the service's principal connection to the Internet. Remember the following two points:

- Other people will, in general, need your CompuServe ID number (such as 74456,312) to send you mail on the Internet. Although, inside CIS, these numbers are always written with a comma between them, you must replace the comma with a period for communication over the Internet.

- You can send e-mail to your pals at other Internet e-mail addresses simply by putting INTERNET: as the first part of the address in response to the address prompt in CompuServe mail, as in

    INTERNET:chseiter@crl.com

You can also get messages out to people who are technically on BITNET or other services, too, at the expense of a little more typing, as in

    INTERNET:SteveM@EDUWXY.BITNET

The e-mail facilities, especially as displayed in CompuServe Navigator, are better than average for national online services.

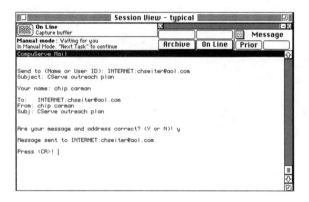

Unlike the other services, CIS can handle Godzilla e-mail files. (AOL's limit is 32K, and Prodigy has special problems.) That means that the time-honored Internet gimmicks of implementing Archie and FTP by e-mail work fairly well. Although I discuss this process a bit back in Part IV, I'll review the details here.

Doing an Archie search by mail

The basic move for doing an Archie search if you're using a service that doesn't have an Archie utility yet is to send an e-mail message to a remote computer that's been specially set up as an Internet server. The remote computer acts on your commands and sends a file back to you as an e-mail message.

1. To search for a file called DOG.TXT, send an e-mail message just like this:

```
To: INTERNET:archie@archie.sura.net
Subject:
prog dog.txt

.
```

2. Put nothing in the Subject line, type the second line just as it appears, and put a period on the last line.

3. To learn how to do fancy Archie searches, send an e-mail message to `archie-l@cs.mcgill.ca` and politely request the file `archie.man.txt`. Better yet, look for this file in CompuServe's own Internet libraries.

It may take a few days before you get your Archie file back by return mail. If you haven't asked for something very specific (don't try `prog mac`, for example), the file will be huge. But the results will tell you where to find the file at least.

Doing an FTP transfer by mail

FTP by mail is more or less the same process.

1. If the Archie search said that DOG.TXT can be found at `ftp.univxyz.edu` and that it's 150K in size, send an e-mail message as follows:

```
TO:INTERNET:ftp.univxyz.edu
Subject:pixie.hqx


reply 71354.341@compuserve.com
connect ftp.univxyz.edu
chunksize 49000
get pixie.hqx
quit
```

The expression `71354.34` here is just standing in for your own CompuServe number with a period instead of a comma. `Chunksize` makes the file segments acceptable to CIS.

2. Download the e-mail files to your own Mac through CompuServe mail by mailing them to yourself.

3. Take each e-mail message into a word processor and strip off the mailing information.

If you got a file in .HQX format, which occurs fairly frequently, you add the chunks together to have one big file of gibberish lines with lots of ASCII punctuation marks and no spaces between the lines. You then unpack the .HQX file by using StuffIt Lite, which you can download from CompuServe.

Some files require special treatment. If you're serious about FTP-by-mail, go into the CompuServe Internet forum libraries and simply download everything you can find about FTP and read it off-line. Plenty of Internet material will call for processing with the program UUENCODE. Don't worry if you don't feel like going through this bit of post-graduate education in Internetica—CompuServe should have worked out a better procedure.

Newsgroups

Newsgroup access in CompuServe is pretty effortless. In fact, the steps of a step-by-step approach are built into the service.

1. Choose Go under the Services menu and type USENET. You get this set of choices:

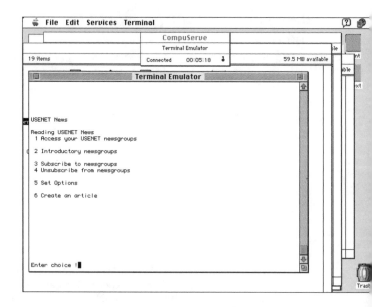

Look at sample newsgroups to get a feeling for how this process works. CompuServe shows you a random assortment of recent articles.

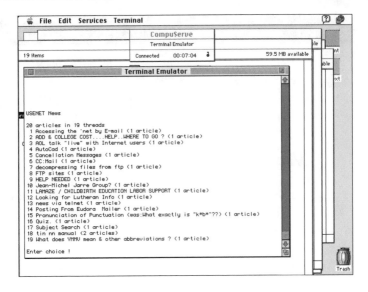

2. After you're in a listing of newsgroups, you can pick a group, which automatically starts you reading the first article.

   CompuServe gives you another menu for actions inside a newsgroup.

```
USENET News

Choices
 1 REPLY
 2 REPLY with Quotation
 3 MAIL
 4 CREATE an article
 5 CANCEL article

 6 REREAD this article
 7 HOLD this article
 8 NEXT article
 9 NEXT THREAD
10 PARENT article

11 CLEAR articles in this newsgroup
12 IGNORE
13 DOWNLOAD this article




Enter choice !
```

How it rates

CompuServe is not a great Internet service, but it's an interesting alternative to the Internet. It has such a huge collection of files and so many subscribers that it offers a lot of what people think they will find when they get on the Internet. The marketing decision to sell "real Internet" services to businesses actually makes fundamental sense, but CompuServe may be swimming against the tide of history. Everyone wants Internet, and other services will be happy to provide it.

Delphi

For more than a year, Delphi has been filling the back covers of computer magazines with an offer for a five-hour, free "Explore the Internet!" service. What makes this remarkable, given that Delphi operates in a world where "Internet access!" in an ad can often mean a badly designed e-mail interface and nothing more, is that Delphi delivers the goods, albeit with a plain-text interface.

What you get

Delphi simply has the goods. Although you reach it with an ordinary terminal communication program (a real-Mac interface is scheduled for late 1994), you get the following:

- E-mail
- Telnet
- FTP and Archie
- Gopher
- Newsgroups
- World Wide Web (text-based)

Using Delphi for the Internet

Delphi's Internet system uses a plain menu, so all you have to be able to do is type out responses to menu prompts. The first menu you see when you sign on lists Internet as a choice; when you thus type **internet** at this menu, you see the following screen.

You then see the Internet menu.

```
Internet SIG Menu:


About the Internet      Help
Conference              Exit
Databases (Files)
EMail                   FTP
Forum (Messages)        Gopher
Guides (Books)          IRC-Internet Relay Chat
Register/Cancel         Telnet
Who's Here              Utilities (finger, traceroute, ping)
Workspace               Usenet Newsgroups
```

Telnet, Archie, FTP, and e-mail

These are all just plain-text versions of the services, much like
you would find in a Unix shell account. The difference is that
Delphi has set up a proper menu structure so that when you pick
one of these items from the menu, you are presented with
another set of choices. You never have to keep a command set in
mind because at every point you have a selection to make,
accompanied by directions. This FTP screen is typical of the
structure of these services.

```
Internet SIG>Enter your selection: ftp
Enter destination INTERNET address: sumex-aim.stanford.edu
Enter username (default: anonymous): anonymous

To get a binary file, type: BINARY and then GET "remote filename" myfilename
To get a text file, type:   ASCII  and then GET "remote filename" myfilename
  Upper and lower case ARE significant; use the "quotes" shown above.
To get a directory, use DIR.
To type a short text file, use TT for myfilename
To get out, type EXIT or Control-Z.

Enter password [XXYYZZ@DELPHI.COM]: XXYYZZ@DELPHI.COM
220 SUMEX-AIM FTP server (Version 4.223 Thu Jun 24 16:42:58 PST 1994) ready.
331 Guest login ok, send mail address (user@host) as password.
230 Guest connection accepted. Restrictions apply.
FTP> ls

200 PORT command successful.
150 Opening ASCII mode data connection for /bin/ls.
info-mac
226 Transfer complete.
```

Gopher and WWW

Delphi has fabricated an interesting arrangement of Gopher and other
searching services. Here's how to find information on any topic
you need:

1. Choose Gopher at the main Internet menu.

    This gets you a list of Gophers for specialized topics and, in true Internet style, links you to all the other Gophers in the world.

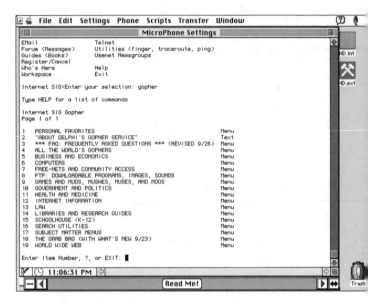

2. Pick the last choice in the Gopher menu.

    You have a functional if austere browser for the WWW. Actually, because Delphi supports 14.4 Kps modem speeds, a text-based browser on Delphi is one of the fastest ways to extract WWW information. It's an exceptionally rich resource (you can even get the plain-vanilla version of the famous NCSA home page).

```
WORLD WIDE WEB
Page 1 of 2

1    Type Any URL                                                    WWW/Web
2    URL FAQ                                                         Text
3    Britannica Online                                              WWW/Web
4    November Eclipse Information                                    WWW/Web
5    Global Network Navigator                                       WWW/Web
6    Guide to Web Weavers                                           WWW/Web
7    EnviroWeb                                                      WWW/Web
8    Games Domain - Games related information site                  WWW/Web
9    Guide to New Users by Steve Franklin                           WWW/Web
10   Info from CERN                                                 WWW/Web
11   Infobot Hotlist Database                                       WWW/Web
12   Interactive Employment Network                                 WWW/Web
13   Interesting Business Sites on the Web                          WWW/Web
14   Internet Business Center                                       WWW/Web
15   The InterNIC InfoGuide Home Page                               WWW/Web
16   Library of Congress World Wide Web Home Page                   WWW/Web
17   NCSA Home Page                                                 WWW/Web
18   Plugged In (educ. programs for low-income communities)         WWW/Web
19   Random Site                                                    WWW/Web

Enter Item Number, MORE, ?, or BACK: █
```

Delphi Internet resources

Instead of going directly to the Internet conference, at the opening menu type **computing** and then type **mac**.

Pick INT from the menu. This set of commands leads you to the following list of choices:

```
Macintosh ICONtact Gopher
Page 1 of 1

1    PERSONAL FAVORITES                      Menu
2    A DIRECT FTP INTERNET CONNECTION        Menu
3    ABOUT DELPHI'S GOPHER SERVICE           Text
4    ARCHIVES OF MAC FILES                   Menu
5    DOCUMENTATION, ETC FOR MACS             Menu
6    FAQ'S, MAC INFO, HELP FOR YOUR MAC      Menu
7    FONTS FOR THE MAC                       Menu
8    GRAPHICS OF ALL FLAVORS                 Menu
9    INTERNET SEARCH UTILITIES               Menu
10   MAC BBS'S ON INTERNET                   Menu
11   MACINTOSH TELNET SITES                  Menu
12   MISC. FILES FOR THE MAC                 Menu
13   PRODUCT INFO ON MACS                    Menu
14   TOOLS FOR YOUR MAC                      Menu
15   UTILITIES FOR YOUR MAC                  Menu
16   WEATHER INFORMATION                     Menu
17   DELPHI'S MAIN GOPHER (INTERNET SIG)     Menu
```

You can save yourself plenty of time and frustration by looking through this section before looking on the Internet. And if you must look, check out item 11 on the list, which records every Mac software archive worth knowing. Another Delphi information resource is HytelNet, a HyperCard stack with a catalog of sites. (It's in the TOOLS&UTILITIES area of DATABASES in the Mac interest group.)

How it rates

The interface isn't spectacular, but this service has the content — all of it. It's more useful for most Mac users than a traditional shell account, and the Macintosh is a big part of Delphi instead of an afterthought. Take the free trial offer and see for yourself!

GEnie

GEnie has done something that all the other on-line services should have done: It hired people to process your Internet requests. Sounds simple enough, and it works just fine. This section doesn't have much step-by-step advice like the AOL section, because there's only one step. You send e-mail to the Internet operators, and they send you what you want. If you're just starting out on the Net, having someone with lots of experience to do your searching for you is an excellent advantage.

What you get

- E-mail
- Archie and FTP
- Gopher
- Internet information

Using GEnie for the Internet

If you are a GEnie user and you're interested in an Internet topic, you send an e-mail message to the system operators of the Internet Roundtable. They do whatever searching is required in Archie, fetch some files for you with FTP, or check out your request with Gopher, and then they send you back the whole package. If you like, you can ask them to forward you the search transcript so you can see how the search was formulated. After you collect a dozen or so of these search transcripts to inspect, you'll understand how to do a search yourself.

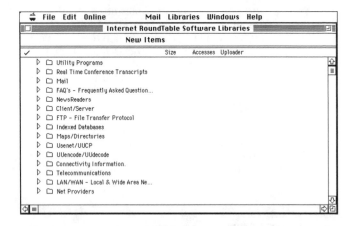

This plan has many advantages. You can send a message to the sysops (system operators) at GEnie, and even if it contains typos, outright misspellings (horrors!), or fairly vague descriptions of what you want, you'll get something useful back. Try this at the standard interface on a Unix-based Internet server, and you're likely to get error messages that you can't even read.

A user with two weeks of hands-on experience is smarter than the best interface artificial-intelligence design can produce. Placing an experienced Internet user between new users and the machines on the Net reduces the frustration level for everyone. Channeling requests to sysops who can access the Internet at odd hours (they *pay* them to do this) greatly relieves traffic problems. Instead of GEnie putting 100 newbies (new users) on the Net at four in the afternoon, the whole GEnie network generates managed bursts of access late at night.

E-Mail basics

Like all other national services, you can send and receive Internet e-mail at GEnie. It's just a bit different from what you might expect.

- Incoming mail should be sent to
  `yourname@genie.geis.com`.

  The `.geis` part is essential because General Electric manages more than one network. Sending a message to `genie.com` won't work.

- Outgoing mail has a funny address inside GEnie. To reach my old mailbox, for example, you would address the letter like so:

  `TO:chseiter@crl.com@INET#`

  Note the *two* @ symbols in the address.

Internet files

GEnie's library is second to none, and you can fetch appropriate files simply by using the lovely point-and-click menu shown in the preceding figure. The snag is that although you can download a USENET newsreader, for example, you can't use it here.

How it rates

GEnie's Mac interface is still rough in spots, but if GEnie can combine its program of providing sysop assistance for new Internet users with direct Internet access and this real-Mac front end, it will be the red-hot service it claims to be in its ads. If your main interest in the Internet is collecting information and files rather than cruising per se, GEnie can get you the goods faster than any other service.

Prodigy

Unlike CompuServe, Prodigy eventually aims to bring more Internet services to regular old civilian subscribers (more than 2 million of them). They're doing this fairly slowly and reluctantly, partly because Prodigy is a determinedly family-oriented service, while the Internet, along with mountains of serious resources, also contains the raunchiest trash that this civilization can produce. Keeping weird files from the hands of the kiddies is a big Prodigy priority.

Despite its slow motion on Internet issues, it's a huge and highly evolved service. It also has a fully graphical interface, even if it doesn't look exactly like a typical Mac screen.

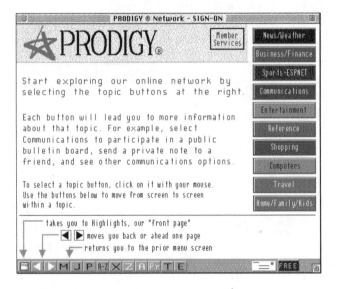

What you get

Prodigy gives you the following:

- E-mail, with some cost restrictions
- An Internet forum
- Newsgroups
- FTP mail services and a book (!) about them

Using Prodigy for the Internet

Here's a rundown of the basic services.

E-Mail

The following screen shows you Prodigy's rather unique on-line
message entry system, which you can use for Internet e-mail.

Use the little pencil icon as the text insertion point. Note that you
have to click to get to the next screen when you have a few
hundred characters in this frame (it doesn't scroll). The process
is a bit slow, but at least you can compose mail off-line to send
later. You can send mail to other people at standard Internet
addresses, but note that inbound mail to you must be addressed
with your Prodigy ID, typically a character/number combination
such as MKRY53A. That is, your Internet pals will have to send
mail to MKRY53A@prodigy.com rather than
cseiter@prodigy.com.

FTP by e-mail, again

Prodigy has a whole 50-page on-line book about doing Archie and
FTP by e-mail. It's geared toward the Prodigy user specifically,
which is nice. That unfortunately means that it's explicitly for PC

users and not Mac users — it's full of references to file types and programs you're not likely to know. If you've used a PC, you know what it means to unPKZIP a file and get to an .EXE executable. The reason you have a Macintosh is to avoid the need for this information.

A separate problem with this approach to Internet service on Prodigy is that Prodigy has an elaborate fee structure for individual incoming messages. A file that has to be broken into six pieces will be fairly expensive by Internet standards.

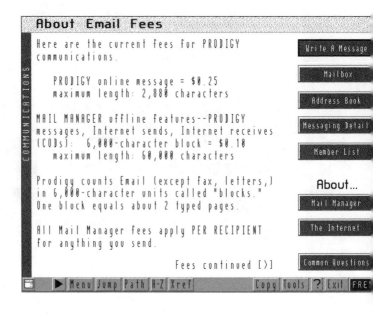

Internet forum

At the main Prodigy screen, one of the menu choices is Jump. If you pick Jump and fill in **Internet** as your choice, you land in the Internet forum, an area undergoing rapid change, as you can see in the next figure.

This area is mostly useful for finding resources (the book on FTP-by-mail, for example) and hints of upcoming features. The bulletin boards are fairly lively, especially in discussion of features that Internet-aware users are demanding.

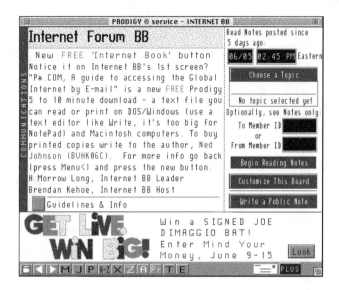

Newsgroups

Prodigy has done a commendable job of adding USENET facilities. You can Jump directly to Internet and click the USENET button to see this screen:

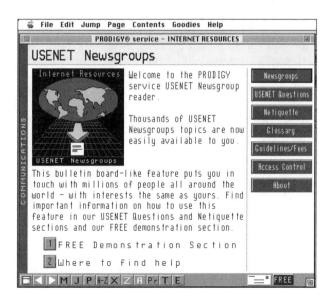

If you click the button for Access Control, you see a manifestation of Prodigy's concern for family orientation. Nonetheless, you can access most USENET newsgroups after you give yourself access permission just by clicking the appropriate self-explanatory buttons.

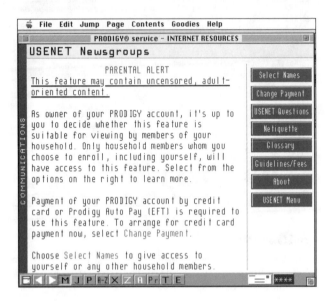

```
 File   Edit   Jump   Page   Contents   Goodies   Help
══════════════ PRODIGY® service – INTERNET RESOURCES ══════════════
  USENET  Newsgroups

              PARENTAL ALERT
     This feature may contain uncensored, adult-        Select Names
     oriented content.
                                                        Change Payment
     As owner of your PRODIGY account, it's up to
     you to decide whether this feature is             USENET Questions
     suitable for viewing by members of your
     household. Only household members whom you          Netiquette
     choose to enroll, including yourself, will
     have access to this feature. Select from the         Glossary
     options on the right to learn more.
                                                       Guidelines/Fees
     Payment of your PRODIGY account by credit
     card or Prodigy Auto Pay (EFT) is required to        About
     use this feature. To arrange for credit card
     payment now, select Change Payment.                USENET Menu

     Choose Select Names to give access to
     yourself or any other household members.
 ◄ ► M J P A-Z X Z A Pr T E                          ═══  ****
```

How it rates

If Prodigy decides what it really wants to do about Internet access, the results could be spectacular — it has the resources to do a good job, and it has a huge user base. So far, it's making progress — but not as fast as AOL.

Let's hope that this organization does everything that Internet forum moderator Brendan Kehoe (*Zen and the Art of the Internet*) suggests it can.

Part VIII

Business Resources

Nothing compares to the explosion of business interest in the World Wide Web. The California Gold Rush of 1849 was a Sunday afternoon children's badminton tournament by comparison. One day in spring 1994, simply nothing was there but a few statistical resources, and then a few months later, a whole globe-spanning system of commerce was in place.

For all practical purposes, *business Internet* means the World Wide Web and graphical browsers (see Appendix VI). Of course, businesses also use e-mail, but that's taken for granted. Major businesses (shown in the next two figures) and now thousands of mom-and-pop enterprises are scrambling to establish a Web presence. This part is a quick guide to establishing your own business on the Web. It's probably going to be valid through most of 1995 — after that, things will be even easier!

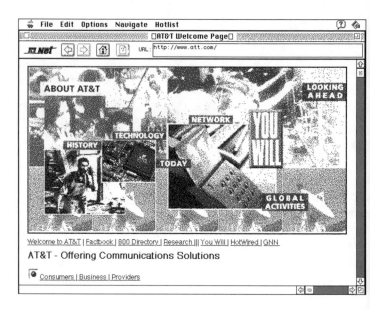

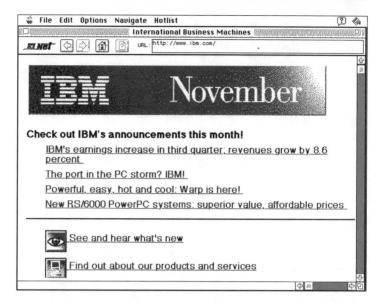

Check out IBM's announcements this month!

IBM's earnings increase in third quarter; revenues grow by 8.6 percent

The port in the PC storm? IBM!

Powerful, easy, hot and cool: Warp is here!

New RS/6000 PowerPC systems: superior value, affordable prices

See and hear what's new

Find out about our products and services

Getting There Yourself

1. Find an Internet provider that can give you a SLIP connection and connect according to the advice in Appendix A.

   Sorry, but there's no other way at the moment. In six or seven months, you will probably be able to look up companies in the standard phone company yellow pages that will show up and do everything for you.

2. Make a SLIP connection to your provider and fire up your copy of MacWeb (or Mosaic, if you have it).

   The great advantage of MacWeb is that it doesn't automatically download all graphics (you double-click the graphics icons to open them). ATT's little exercise in corporate vanity (the first figure in this part) will cost you about five minutes on a 9600 bps modem.

3. When you have MacWeb running, choose Open URL from the File menu.

4. In the URL space, type **http://www.openmarket.com/**.

   You see an OpenMarket home page like that in the following figure after you unpack all the little icons.

Looking Around

1. Click the button for Commercial Sites Index.

   Doing so allows you to check out the other businesses that are already present on the Web. This takes you to the site `http://www/directory/net/`, which has both an indexed directory you can search and a very hot What's New page.

2. It's almost futile to attempt to describe what you find when you get here; with the rate of addition of new material means in a given week, the What's New section should list several hundred businesses. You may want to search for particular topics (there's a search link on the home page) rather than scroll through the whole thing.

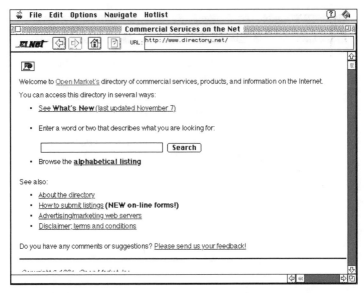

3. One of the things you can find here, if you like, is yourself. On the home page for www.directory.net is a link to a Listing form. You can list your own company with its e-mail address so that it appears in future Internet directories.

File Edit Options Navigate Hotlist

Listing Submission

URL: http://www.directory.net/dir/submit.cgi

Listing Submission

You can use this form to submit new listings, updates, and announcements to the Commercial Sites Index. This form replaces the old method of submitting listings with e-mail.

Please list companies, institutions, or organizations, **not** individual products or services. Please follow the guidelines, and read our the terms and conditions.

Do you have any questions or suggestions about our listing submission process? Please send us your comments.

Please give your e-mail address so we can reach you if there are problems with the listing:

Your e-mail address:

Is this an update for an existing listing or a new listing? For updates, please enter only the information that needs to be updated. For new listings, please enter all requested fields:

- ● New listing
- ○ Updated listing

Give the name for the listing (e.g. "Fred's Carwash, Inc."):

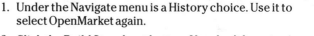

Signing Up

1. Under the Navigate menu is a History choice. Use it to select OpenMarket again.

2. Click the Build Storefront button. You don't have to sign up right now — this is just to show you how it's done.

3. You see a page of the type shown in the following figure. You can step through the process of creating your own Internet storefront.

4. If you want to see what a storefront on the Internet looks like, click one of the sample store links. You don't have to understand HTML to do so — OpenMarket provides a standard set of forms.

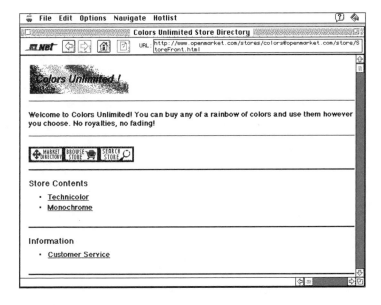

A question that you may have at this point is: how much does this cost? In late 1994, the answer to this question looks like the following figure.

```
Introductory pricing:

Open Market offers three tiers of *introductory* pricing for the
StoreBuilder kit and ongoing monthly fees (rent) for merchants,
depending on the amount of information contained in each store:

Level             Store Size           Set-Up Fee   Monthly Charge
Kiosk(*)     1 MB (approx. 20 pages)     $300           $50
Standard     5 MB (approx. 50 pages)     $500           $75
Premiere         more than 5 MB         $1500          $300

These prices are subject to change after our introductory period and
do not include either payment transaction fees, or charges for additional
storage requirements.

(*) Kiosk merchants do not have access to
Open Market's payment system.
```

Using the Global Network Navigator and Other Resources

Another place to point your copy of MacWeb is the Global Network Navigator, a product of O'Reilly and Associates, which is a pioneering Internet virtual firm and publisher of numerous early UNIX-based Internet books.

You can get to the GNN with the URL `http://www.gnn.com/`.

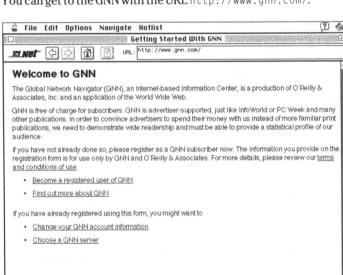

The GNN business page is a premier location for finding Internet-oriented businesses, and under its business services section you can find a number of firms that are ready and waiting to help you sign onto the Web.

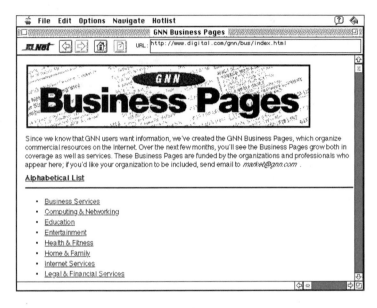

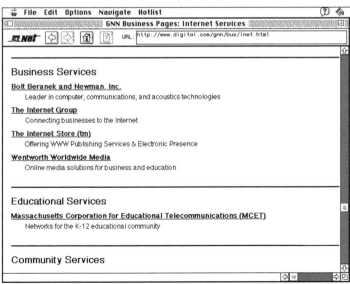

Finally, here's an assortment of business Web sites for you to inspect. Everyone has a variety of services, and you may want to shop around among them when you're looking for a home for your own business. (For a more complete listing, see Appendix D.)

- **intergroup.com** (3 listings)
- **www.baynet.com** (3 listings)
- **www.primenet.com** (3 listings)
- **www.interaccess.com** (3 listings)
- **www.neosoft.com** (3 listings)
- **www.iquest.net** (3 listings)
- **www.venture.net** (3 listings)
- **www.rai.com** (3 listings)
- **www.comnet.com** (3 listings)
- **www.enet.net** (3 listings)
- **sparky.cyberzine.org** (3 listings)
- **gnn.com** (3 listings)
- **www.netmarket.com** (3 listings)
- **www.elpress.com** (3 listings)
- **www.cs.colorado.edu** (3 listings)
- **envirolink.org** (3 listings)
- **www.digex.net** (3 listings)
- **www.solutionsrc.com** (3 listings)
- **www.awa.com** (3 listings)
- **www.commerce.digital.com** (3 listings)

IDG selected TCP Connect II to include with the *Internet For Macs For Dummies Starter Kit* (see Chapter 7) because InterCon's setup procedure is simpler than most: It installs MacTCP and InterSLIP for you. If you decide not to use TCP Connect II after the free trial period in that package, you will still have MacTCP and InterSLIP on your computer and can then attempt to use other shareware (Fetch, TurboGopher, and Mosaic) to get an Internet connection running.

Boarding the Internet

This section is for individuals who are willing to find a service provider that offers SLIP accounts and who will be contacting the service with a modem. That's a "dial-up SLIP" account, in case your friends ask you.

 Don't do any of this as your introduction to the Internet. Instead, do some practicing with Pipeline or take one of the inevitable free offers from America Online.

1. Go to the Macintosh software archives on Pipeline or AOL and get your own copies of Fetch and TurboGopher.

 You may also want to collect the information files on MacTCP. Check to make sure that you're running your modem at its highest speed, because these files take a while to download.

2. Check your configuration.

If you ran the InterCon installer with the *Internet For Macs For Dummies Starter Kit,* you already have copies of MacTCP and InterSLIP in your System folder, but now you should check your configuration again. Note that MacTCP is simply included in System 7.5. If you didn't buy the Starter Kit and don't have System 7.5, you may have to get MacTCP from Apple. It's cheaper to get the Starter Kit.

3. Find a SLIP provider.

IDG has included coupons at the back of the Starter Kit for SLIP providers, including CRL, my own home site. If you don't like the companies in the coupons, look in *Boardwatch Magazine* or *Online Access* and leaf through the ads; new players appear in this game almost weekly. A local version of the tabloid computer monthly *Microtimes* is another good place to look, as you can find it for free at newsstands in big cities. Just look for the word *SLIP*.

Expect a setup fee and then monthly fees between $15 and $25. However, it's also typical not to have a per-hour charge. When you call about getting an account, ask for the Customer Support number. Then call Customer Support and ask the operator if he or she is familiar with MacTCP and InterSLIP. Some services do ten Mac setups a day, and some can't be bothered. You want one that *will* bother. And get a fax number, which you'll need to get configured.

4. Put MacTCP (when you get it) in the Control Panels folder of your System folder. InterSLIP has a Control Panels folder, too, called InterSLIP Control, which also goes in your System folder.

5. Make photocopies of the following figures.

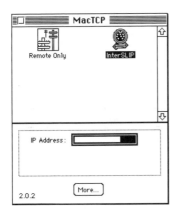

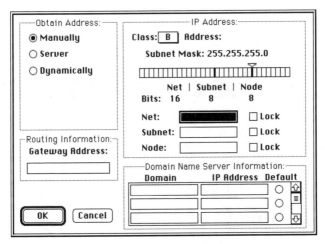

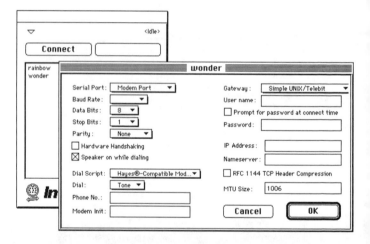

Configuring

Before following these steps, photocopy the figures as instructed in the section "Boarding the Internet."

1. Fax these figures to Customer Support at your service provider.

2. Tell Support to fill in the right numbers in the blank spaces.

3. Ask Support to show you where to set the little slider for Subnet Mask in the second figure.

4. Have Support fax the whole set of figures back to you with all this information marked on the faxes.

5. Find Control Panels under the Apple menu and double-click to open it. Find the MacTCP icon and double-click it.

   If you don't see an InterSLIP icon as shown in the first figure under "Boarding the Internet," then you haven't put the InterSLIP parts (Control Panels and Extension) in the right places. Do that now, and then come back and type the IP Address.

6. Double-click the More... button. Fill in the information that Support gave you for the first figure. Make sure that you have the Obtain Address button set properly and move the Subnet Mask slider to the position Support recommended. Fill in the Domain Name Server data in the lower right and pick the default.

7. You may have a version of SLIP that shows nothing in the scrolling list area yet. Just pick New from the File menu and fill in a name in the dialog box.

   After you're done, click back to the window in the third figure and double-click your new filename, which brings you to a screen that looks like the fourth figure.

Connecting

Before following these steps, you need to photocopy the figures as instructed in the section "Boarding the Internet."

1. For Gateway, pick Simple UNIX/Telebit (because you're not a direct connection). Pick Hayes... under Dial Script and then pick your modem's speed.

   Every other bit of information should be on the fax you got back for the fourth figure.

2. Double-click the InterSLIP Setup icon to get to a window like that in the third figure. Click the Connect button.

   InterSLIP makes your connection.

3. Watch the top of the window.

   The message changes from Idle to Dialing and then to Signing In and Connected. Sometimes you see it pop back to Idle. It's a good idea to check the Speaker on box in the fourth figure so that you can hear whether your dial-up number is busy or whether (as often happens) no line is available (in which case, you'd again hear a busy signal).

4. When InterSLIP says that you're connected, double-click your version of MacWeb or Mosaic and you're on the World Wide Web!

You can also use Fetch or TurboGopher, but you can use only one program at a time.

Appendix B

Hot Internet Sites

FTP Hotspots

Reach these either with the TCP software in the *Internet For Macs For Dummies Starter Kit,* through Fetch, or through plain old Unix FTP (see Part IV). These sites are all repositories of the most-sought-after Mac files.

mac.archive.umich.edu	141.211.32.2	/mac
sumex-aim.stanford.edu	36.44.0.6	/info-mac
ftp.apple.com	130.43.2.3	/dts
ftp.ncsa.uiuc.edu	141.142.20.50	/Mac (Mosaic)
ftp.funet.fi	128.214.6.100	/pub/mac
ftp.dartmouth.edu	129.170.16.54	/pub/mac (Dartmouth)
boombox.micro.umn.edu	128.101.95.95	/pub (gopher, more)
ftp.rrzn.uni-hannover.de(*)	130.75.2.2	/ftp1/mac [sumex]
ftp.ucs.ubc.ca(*)	137.82.27.62	/pub/mac/ info-mac
shark.mel.dit.csiro.au(*)	144.110.16.11	/info-mac [sumex]

World Wide Web Hotspots

Remember, to get to a Web site, you type in these HTTP addresses in the Open URL...dialog box under the File menu in your browser, like so:

```
http://galaxy.einet.net/
```

or

```
http://www.ncsa.uiuc.edu/
```

or

```
http://www.cyfer.net/
```

```
www.commerce.net
```

CommerceNet is an aggressively expanding business society based in Silicon Valley.

```
www.geo.net
```

This address is the new site name for `www.global.net`, a large mixed-bag resource. The subdivision `www.geo.net:8210` has piles of catalogs, for example, while `www.geo.net:8510/heart.html/` is an on-line job-search forum.

```
web.cnam.fr
```

These people would like to help you put your own business on the Web.

```
www.cix.org
```

The CIX acronym stands for Commerce Internet Exchange. Stop here to pick up background information on making your own business Net-aware.

```
www.ncsa.uiuc.edu
```

The second-to-last bit stands for University of Illinois, Urbana-Champaign.

```
tns-www.lcs.mit.edu
```

Check in here to find out how to make up your own host page — they've got a kit for you to use.

```
www.well.sf.ca.us
```

Take a look at the future of private local computer organizations on the Web.

The Alt newsgroups arose as a way to distinguish popular topics from the original core topics (physics, math, computer science, and other serious matters) in the USENET universe. They loom large in the mythology of the Internet, because they're where the fun is, among other things.

This list is a severely edited version of a list posted regularly to a newsgroup called news.lists, which you can join from any Internet provider that offers USENET newsgroups. The list is maintained by a volunteer named David C. Lawrence (Internet address tale@uunet.uu.net), who is thus the person to notify when groups are created or disappear. It's another example of the remarkable way the Internet operates — the list is a key piece of information about the Internet, and it's not under the control of an organization or business.

If you want the full version of the list, you should download it yourself. The complete list has topics and descriptions that are too X-rated for this little fun-for-the-whole-family book, and there's also an amazing amount of repetition — very similar topics often appear in three or four separate newsgroups.

Social Issues

This list is about one-fourth of the social-issue groups on USENET. Different types of activist communities staked out their turf fairly early in Internet history.

alt.abuse.recovery	Helping victims of abuse to recover.
alt.activism	Activities for activists.
alt.activism.d	A place to discuss issues in alt.activism.
alt.activism.death-penalty	For people opposed to capital punishment.
alt.adoption	For those involved with or contemplating adoption.
alt.child-support	Raising children in a split family.
alt.censorship	Discussion about restricting speech/press.
alt.current-events.bosnia	The strife of Bosnia-Herzegovina.
alt.current-events.clinton.whitewater	The Clinton Whitewater Scandal.

`alt.current-events.russia`	Current happenings in Russia.
`alt.current-events.usa`	What's new in the United States.
`alt.dads-rights`	Rights of fathers. (Moderated)
`alt.discrimination`	Quotas, affirmative action, bigotry, persecution.
`alt.education.disabled`	Education for people with physical/mental disabilities.
`alt.education.distance`	Learning from teachers who are far away.
`alt.feminism`	Like `soc.feminism`, only different.
`alt.fraternity.sorority`	Discussions of fraternity/sorority life and issues.
`alt.individualism`	Philosophies where individual rights are paramount.
`alt.missing-kids`	Locating missing children.
`alt.parents-teens`	Parent-teenager relationships.
`alt.politics.greens`	Green party politics & activities worldwide.
`alt.politics.usa.constitution`	U.S. Constitutional politics.
`alt.recovery`	For people in recovery programs (e.g., AA, ACA, GA).
`alt.recovery.codependency`	Mutually destructive relationships.
`alt.sexual.abuse.`	Helping others deal with traumatic experiences.
`alt.support`	Dealing with emotional situations & experiences.
`alt.support.cancer`	Emotional aid for people with cancer.
`alt.support.depression`	Depression and mood disorders.
`alt.support.divorce`	Discussion of marital breakups.
`alt.support.step-parents`	Helping people with their step-parents.
`alt.support.stuttering`	Support for people who stutter.
`alt.war`	Not just collateral damage.

At the Extremes

These groups contain plenty of interesting speculative material.

alt.alien.visitors	Space Aliens on Earth! Abduction! Gov't Coverup!
alt.conspiracy	Be paranoid — they're out to get you.
alt.out-of-body	Out of Body Experiences.
alt.paranet.skeptic	"I don't believe they turned you into a newt."
alt.paranet.ufo	"Heck, I guess naming it 'UFO' identifies it."
alt.paranormal	Phenomena which are not scientifically explicable.
alt.sci.physics.new-theories	Scientific theories you won't find in journals.

Computer Stuff

Please note that these are discussion groups rather than sources of software. You can, however, get plenty of advice if you want it.

alt.bbs.internet	BBSs that are hooked up to the Internet.
alt.best.of.internet	It was a time of sorrow, it was a time of joy.
alt.gopher	Discussion of the Gopher information service.
alt.irc.questions	How-to questions for IRC (International Relay Chat).
alt.lang.basic	The Language That Would Not Die.
alt.online-service	Large commercial on-line services, and the Internet.
alt.online-service.america-online	Discussions and questions about America Online.
alt.online-service.compuserve	Discussions and questions about CompuServe.
alt.online-service.delphi	Discussions and questions about Delphi.

alt.online-service.freenet	Public FreeNet systems.
alt.online-service.prodigy	The Prodigy system.
alt.sources.mac	Source file newsgroup for the Apple Macintosh computers.

Critters

I expect that as more dog and cat owners get on the Internet, there will be postings of upcoming shows and the like. It's pretty hard to believe there's a skunks group and not at least one for Persian cat fanciers.

alt.animals.badgers	Badgers (meles meles and others).
alt.animals.dolphins	Flipper, Darwin, and all their friends.
alt.animals.foxes	Everything you ever wanted to know about vulpines.
alt.aquaria	The aquarium & related as a hobby.
alt.fan.lemurs	Little critters with BIG eyes.
alt.pets.rabbits	Coneys abound.
alt.skunks	Enthusiasts of skunks and other mustelidae.
alt.wolves	Discussing wolves & wolf-mix dogs.

Games

There are more groups actually playing games on the Internet than discussing them.

alt.anagrams	Playing with words.
alt.games.mtrek	Multi-Trek, a multi-user Star Trek-like game.
alt.games.netrek.paradise	Discussion of the paradise version of netrek.
alt.games.video.classic	Video games from before the mid-1980s.
alt.sega.genesis	Another addiction.
alt.super.nes	Like rec.games.video.nintendo, only different.

Sports

I'm only listing a few of the groups for professional sports teams. Your favorite team is almost certainly listed, in the same format as these, as `alt.sports.<sports>.<team-name>`.

`alt.archery`	Robin Hood had the right idea.
`alt.caving`	Spelunk.
`alt.fishing`	Like `rec.outdoors.fishing`, only different.
`alt.skate-board`	Discussion of all apsects of skate-boarding.
`alt.sport.bowling`	In the gutter again.
`alt.sport.darts`	Look what you've done to the wall!
`alt.sport.falconry`	The taking of live game by using a trained raptor.
`alt.sport.jet-ski`	Discussion of personal watercraft.
`alt.sport.officiating`	Problems related to officiating athletic contests.
`alt.sport.pool`	Knock your balls into your pockets for fun.
`alt.sport.racquetball`	All aspects of indoor racquetball and related sports.
`alt.sport.squash`	With the proper technique, vegetables can go very fast.
`alt.sports.baseball.chicago-cubs`	Chicago Cubs major league baseball.
`alt.sports.basketball.nba.la-lakers`	Los Angeles Lakers NBA basketball.
`alt.sports.college.ivy-league`	Ivy League athletics.
`alt.sports.football.mn-vikings`	Minnesota Vikings football talk.
`alt.sports.football.pro.gb-packers`	Green Bay Packers NFL football talk.
`alt.sports.hockey.nhl.tor-mapleleafs`	Toronto Maple Leafs NHL hockey talk.
`alt.surfing`	Riding the ocean waves.

Fan Clubs

This listing represents roughly 8 percent of the fan-club material on the lists. These were selected for no other reason than personal eccentricity.

alt.books.anne-rice	The vampire stuff.
alt.elvis.king	You've heard of this guy.
alt.fan.blues-brothers	Jake & Elwood ride again!
alt.fan.disney.afternoon	Disney Afternoon characters & shows.
alt.fan.hofstadter	Douglas Hofstadter, Godel, Escher, Bach, and others.
alt.fan.howard-stern	Fans of the abrasive radio & TV personality.
alt.fan.jimmy-buffett	A white sports coat and a pink crustacean.
alt.fan.laurie.anderson	Will it be a music concert or a lecture this time?
alt.fan.letterman	One of the top ten reasons to get the alt groups.
alt.fan.noam-chomsky	Noam Chomsky's writings and opinions.
alt.fan.oingo-boingo	Have you ever played ping pong in Pago Pago?
alt.fan.penn-n-teller	The magicians Penn & Teller.
alt.fan.rush-limbaugh	Just what it says.
alt.fan.u2	The Irish rock band U2.
alt.fan.wodehouse	Discussion of the works of humor author P.G. Wodehouse.
alt.fan.woody-allen	The diminutive director.
alt.music.peter-gabriel	Discussion of the music of Peter Gabriel.
alt.ql.creative	The *Quantum Leap* TV show.
alt.tv.barney	He's everywhere. Now appearing in several alt groups.

The Arts, More or Less

This list uses a fairly elastic definition of art.

`alt.artcom`	Artistic Community, arts & communication.
`alt.arts.ballet`	All aspects of ballet & modern dance as performing art.
`alt.binaries.pictures.cartoons`	Images from animated cartoons.
`alt.binaries.pictures.fine-art.d`	Discussion of the fine-art binaries. (Moderated)
`alt.binaries.pictures.fine-art.digitized`	Art from conventional media. (Moderated)
`alt.binaries.pictures.fine-art.graphics`	Art created on computers. (Moderated)
`alt.books.reviews`	"If you want to know how it turns out, read it!"
`alt.folklore.urban`	Urban legends, ala Jan Harold Brunvand.
`alt.guitar`	Strumming and picking.
`alt.magic`	For discussion about stage magic.
`alt.music.a-cappella`	Like `rec.music.a-cappella`, only different.
`alt.music.alternative`	For groups having two or fewer Platinum-selling albums.
`alt.music.blues-traveler`	For "All fellow travelers."
`alt.music.progressive`	Yes, Marillion, Asia, King Crimson …
`alt.music.synthpop`	Depeche Mode, Erasure, Pet Shop Boys, and much more!
`alt.music.techno`	Bring on the bass!
`alt.music.world`	Discussion of music from around the world.
`alt.prose`	Postings of original writings, fictional and otherwise.
`alt.tv.mst3k`	The finest cultural newsgroup on earth (author's opinion)!
`alt.zines`	Small magazines, mostly non-commercial.

Religion

This area is full of many lively discussions. It's sometimes strange to think of comments on ancient manuscripts flying back and forth on high-speed fiber-optic links.

`alt.christnet`	Gathering place for Christian ministers and users.
`alt.christnet.bible`	Bible discussion and research.
`alt.christnet.philosophy`	Philosophical implications of Christianity.
`alt.christnet.theology`	The distinctives of God of Christian theology.
`alt.hindu`	The Hindu religion. (Moderated)
`alt.messianic`	Messianic traditions.
`alt.philosophy.zen`	Zen for everyone.
`alt.religion.christian`	Unmoderated forum for discussing Christianity.
`alt.religion.gnostic`	History and philosophies of the Gnostic sects.
`alt.religion.islam`	Discussion of Islamic Faith & Society.

Funny Business

Humor is a giant newsgroup topic. If you're the only person in Nonesuch, Wyoming who thinks Dave Barry is funny, you can find pals on the Net. In USENET humor newsgroups like `alt.humor.best-of-usenet`, off-color jokes are typically encoded in a simple substitution cipher, so if you go to the trouble of decoding it, you don't have much business complaining about your sensibilities being assaulted.

`alt.comedy.british`	Discussion of British comedy in a variety of media.
`alt.comedy.british.blackadder`	The Black Adder programme.
`alt.comedy.firesgn-thtre`	Firesign Theatre in all its flaming glory.
`alt.comedy.standup`	Discussion of stand-up comedy and comedians.

(continued)

`alt.fan.dave-barry`	Electronic fan club for humorist Dave Barry.
`alt.fan.monty-python`	Electronic fan club for those wacky Brits.
`alt.fan.mst3k`	A forum of incisive cultural comment.
`alt.humor.` `best-of-USENET`	What the moderator thinks is funniest. (Moderated)

Appendix D

WWW and WWW Servers

This is an extract of frequently asked questions about the World Wide Web, followed by a list of servers.

What Are WWW, Hypertext, and Hypermedia?

WWW stands for *World Wide Web*. The WWW project, started by CERN (the European Laboratory for Particle Physics), seeks to build a distributed hypermedia system.

The advantage of hypertext is that in a hypertext document, if you want more information about a particular subject mentioned, you can usually "just click it" to read further details. In fact, documents can be and often are linked to other documents by completely different authors — much like footnoting, but you can get the referenced document instantly!

To access the Web, you run a browser program. The browser reads documents and can fetch documents from other sources. Information providers set up hypermedia servers that browsers can get documents from.

The browsers can, in addition, access files by FTP, NNTP (the Internet news protocol), Gopher, and an ever-increasing range of other methods. On top of these, if the server has search capabilities, the browsers permit searches of documents and databases.

The documents that the browsers display are *hypertext* documents. Hypertext is text with pointers to other text. The browsers let you deal with the pointers in a transparent way — select the pointer, and you are presented with the text that is pointed to.

Hypermedia is a superset of hypertext — it is any medium with pointers to other media. This means that browsers may not display a text file but may display images or sound or animations.

What Is a URL?

URL stands for *Uniform Resource Locator*. It is a draft standard for specifying an object on the Internet, such as a file or newsgroup. URLs look like this:

- `file://wuarchive.wustl.edu/mirrors/msdos/graphics/gifkit.zip`
- `file://wuarchive.wustl.edu/mirrors/`
- `http://info.cern.ch:80/default.html/`

- `news:alt.hypertext`
- `telnet://dra.com/`

The first part of the URL (before the colon) specifies the access method. The part of the URL after the colon is interpreted specific to the access method. In general, two slashes after the colon indicate a machine name (`machine:port` is also valid).

In this appendix, you often see URLs surrounded by angle brackets. I've done so because some newsreaders (I am told) can recognize them and treat them as "buttons." Do not enter the angle brackets when entering a URL by hand to your Web browser.

When you are told to *check out this URL*, what to do next depends on your browser; please check Help for your particular browser. For the line-mode browser at CERN, which you will quite possibly use first via telnet, the command to try a URL is GO *URL* (substitute the actual URL, of course). In Lynx, you just select the "GO" link on the first page you see; in graphical browsers, there's usually an "Open URL" option in the menus.

Telnet-Accessible Browsers

An up-to-date list of these is available on the Web as `http://info.cern.ch/hypertext/WWW/FAQ/Bootstrap.html` and it should be regarded as an authoritative list. Here's a list I've compiled:

`info.cern.ch`

No password is required; this is in Switzerland, so continental U.S. users may be better off using a closer browser.

`ukanaix.cc.ukans.edu`

A full-screen browser Lynx, which requires a vt100 terminal. Log in as `www`.

`www.njit.edu`

(or telnet `128.235.163.2`) a full-screen browser in New Jersey Institute of Technology, USA Log in as `www`.

`vms.huji.ac.il`

(IP address `128.139.4.3`). A dual-language Hebrew/English database with links to the rest of the world; the line mode browser, plus extra features. Hebrew University of Jerusalem, Israel. Log in as `www`.

Macintosh WWW Browsers

Note: All these browsers require that you have SLIP, PPP, or other TCP/IP networking on your PC. SLIP and PPP can be accomplished over phone lines, but only with the active cooperation of your network provider or educational institution. If you only have normal dial-up shell access, your best option at this time is to run Lynx on the system you call.

Mosaic for Macintosh

From NCSA. Full featured; available by anonymous FTP from `ftp.ncsa.uiuc.edu` in the directory Mac/Mosaic.

MacWeb

Available by anonymous FTP from `ftp.galaxy.einet.net`

Netcape

Available by anonymous FTP or `ftp.incom.com`

Samba

From CERN. Basic; available by anonymous FTP from `info.cern.ch` in the directory /ftp/pub/www/bin as the file `mac`.

What Are Information Providers?

Information providers run programs from which the browsers can obtain hypertext. These programs can either be WWW servers that understand the HyperText Transfer Protocol HTTP (best if you are creating your information database from scratch), "gateway" programs that convert an existing information format to hypertext, or a non-HTTP server that WWW browsers can access — anonymous FTP or Gopher, for example.

To learn more about World Wide Web servers, you can consult a WWW server primer by Nathan Torkington, available at the URL

```
<http://www.vuw.ac.nz/who/Nathan.Torkington/
ideas/www-servers.html>.
```

If you only want to provide information to local users, placing your information in local files is also an option. This means, however, that there can be no off-machine access.

Server Information

CERN's server is available for anonymous FTP from `info.cern.ch` and many other places. Use Archie to search for "www" or "WWW" to find copies close to you. NCSA has also released a server, available for FTP from `ftp.ncsa.uiuc.edu`.

There is a server for the Macintosh, MacHTTP, available at the URL

```
<http://www.uth.tmc.edu/mac_info/
machttp_info.html>.
```

For more information on writing servers and gateways in general, see

```
http://info.cern.ch/hypertext/WWW/Daemon/
Overview.html.
```

Making Web Documents in HTML

There are several ways to produce HTML. One is to simply write it by hand; try the "source" button of your browser to look at the HTML for an interesting page. Odds are it'll be a great deal simpler than you would expect. If you're used to marking up text in any way (even red-penciling it), HTML should be rather intuitive. A beginner's guide to HTML is available at the URL

```
<http://www.ncsa.uiuc.edu/General/Internet/
WWW/HTMLPrimer.html>.
```

There is also an HTML primer by Nathan Torkington at the URL

```
<http://www.vuw.ac.nz/who/Nathan.Torkington/
ideas/www-html.html>.
```

Of course, most folks would still prefer to use a friendlier, graphical editor. One option is to use an SGML editor with the HTML DTD. Another, for EMACS fans, is to use EMACS and `html-mode.el`.

In addition, there are two collections of filters for converting your existing documents (in TeX and other non-HTML formats) into HTML automatically:

- Rich Brandwein and Mike Sendall's List at CERN. The URL is

```
<http://info.cern.ch/hypertext/WWW/Tools/
Filters.html>.
```

- NCSA's List of Filters and Editors, which also mentions two editors for MS Windows. The URL is

```
<http://www.ncsa.uiuc.edu/SDG/Software/
Mosaic/Docs/faq-software.html#editors>.
```

What's Out There?

One of the few limitations of the current networked information systems is that no simple way exists to find out what has changed, what is new, or even what is out there. As a result, a definitive list of the Web's contents is impossible at this moment. There are, however, several resources that provide a great deal of information on new and established servers by topic. These are just two:

- The WWW Virtual Library, which is a good place to find resources on a particular subject, is at the URL

```
<http://info.cern.ch/hypertext/DataSources/
bySubject/Overview.html >.
```

- What's New With NCSA Mosaic, which carries announcements of new servers on the web, is at the URL

```
<http://www.ncsa.uiuc.edu/SDG/Software/
Mosaic/Docs/whats-new.html>.
```

More Info

To find out more, use the Web. This FAQ hopefully provides enough information for you to locate and install a browser on your system. If you have system-specific questions regarding FTP, networking, and the like, please consult newsgroups relevant to your particular hardware and operating system!

Later you may return to this FAQ for answers to some of the advanced questions covered in the second section. The advanced section contains the most-asked technical questions in the group.

After you're up and running, you may want to consult the *World Wide Web Primer* by Nathan Torkington. It is available at the URL

```
<http://www.vuw.ac.nz/who/Nathan.Torkington/
ideas/www-primer.html>.
```

Business on the Web

This is a snapshot in time of business activity on the Web. To check out any one of these servers, just go to Open URL under the File menu in your Web browser and type in **http://www.cts.com**, for example, to get the first server in the list. You can also get to http://wws.directory.net/ to make up your own list.

One reason IDG has included this list is to help you decide whether your own business belongs on the Web. If the answer to this question is yes, you'll also find lots of consulting firms in the list who will help you set up your own business page. Good luck!

Listings hosted on **www.cts.com:**

- Absolutely Fresh Flowers
- Body Wise International
- Center for Anxiety and Stress Treatment
- Creative-Leadership Consultants, Inc.
- Datel
- Excel
- Executive Image
- HabitSmart
- HeartPrints
- Historical Interaction
- It's NEW! Magazine
- LAN Performance Labs
- National Consultant Referrals, Inc.
- OKbridge
- Software Products International
- Stock Doctor
- Unarius Academy of Science
- Virtual Entertainment
- Wall Street Direct

If National Consultant Referrals gets you a hot job, tell your friends to send you flowers through Absolutely Fresh Flowers. Later, you can check the Center for Anxiety and Stress Treatment after the consulting job keeps you on airplanes 55 percent of the time.

Listings hosted on **mmink.cts.com:**

- A Aa Building Inspection Services
- Allmakes Office Machines Co., Inc.
- Ann Hemyng Candy, Inc.'s Chocolate Factory
- Cafe Mam-Organically Grown Coffee
- Center for Arthroscopic Surgery
- Costa Travel Online
- Earrings, by Lisa!
- The Earth Pledge Foundation
- Insurance Research Network
- Internet Ad Emporium
- P.DEVELOPMENTS LTD
- Personal Impressions
- Preferred Golf Tours
- Realty Referral Network
- The Sandal Dude
- Scottso The Clown

Except for Insurance Research Network, `mmink.cts.com` is a "fun" Web site. Whenever you have Scottso hanging out with the Sandal Dude, anything can happen!

Listings hosted on **www.globalx.net:**

- Full On Custom Painting
- Global MONITOR Computer Magazine
- Global-X-Change
- Lundy Construction
- Mountain Masters Bicycles
- Network Support Inc.
- North 45 Management Corp.
- Ontario Coalition for Better Cycling
- Ottawa-Carleton Economic Development Corporation
- Ottawa-Carleton Entrepreneurship Centre
- PSS Records and Imaging Software
- Rhonda Francis Communications
- Tai Chi Studio W.T.B.A.

High technology gives rise to some unexpected businesses. Along with some fairly standard Canadian organizations, there are the unique sound and image capabilities of PSS.

Listings hosted on **branch.com:**

- American Employment Weekly
- The Bonsai Boy of New York
- Branch Information Services
- Buning the Florist
- Burpco
- Digital Dynamics
- Forest Hill Vineyard
- Info VID Outlet
- Legacy Group of America
- New World Books
- Stonewall Partners

Once again, here's an odd mix of businesses. The American Employment weekly is worth checking out, and InfoVID has videos that aren't movies (lots of them). Bonsai Boy is self-explanatory, but I don't know about Burpco.

Listings hosted on **www.medium.com:**

- AL Baker's XR's Only
- AMCOL Corporation
- American Consultants League
- AmFax
- Graphic Finishers of America
- THE INTERNET STORE
- Rogers Sewing Center
- Source 1 Travel
- Web Techs
- World Market Development

Go directly to the INTERNET STORE. With each page here, there are often many other pages — this is a good example.

Listings hosted **www.tagsys.com:**

- AMP
- Ariel and Shya Kane, Inc.
- Joshua A. Blau
- Laura A. Blau
- Free Spirit Magazine
- Tamara Jebin Tours
- Diana Kane & Co.
- Science Fiction Shop
- TAG Online Mall

Attorneys can advertise, and they can advertise on the Web. That's what's going on with the names of individuals here. Now, if they could just put up a form where you fill in the information about a case and then collect an on-line jury to review it. . . .

Listings hosted on **www.mountain.net:**

- Barry's Office Service, Inc.
- Davis & Associates
- Family Wholesale Network, Inc.
- Hannah's House
- J & S Business Forms
- Lee Mirabal's Positive Press Newsletter
- Morning Stars Sales
- Stilwell Book Shop
- Teletronics Company

Listings hosted on **www.oslonett.no:**

- Arctic Adventours
- Candle
- EUnet Norway
- Norwegian Library House
- Oslonett, Inc.
- Taskon
- Telepost Communication

At current (and falling) prices, it's cost-effective for individual stores to run their mail-order operations through the Web. Notice the beginnings of more international presence with the `oslonett.no` Norwegian server. You'll see a commercial server for every country here within months.

Listings hosted on **www.webscope.com:**

- ARTrageous
- Fishelp
- Global Leasing Services
- Imperial Copy Products, Inc.
- Long Island, New York
- On Target Marketing
- Premier Staff Ltd.
- Shremagraphs

Listings hosted on **www.biznet.com.blacksburg.va.us:**

- Backstreets
- BizNet Technologies
- Busch Entertainment
- Durability, Inc.
- Home Technologies, Inc.
- Tech Bookstore
- Wade's Grocery

This group is the very definition of mixed bags. BizNet can actually help you, and Wade's Grocery is a harbinger of things to come. There's no reason a grocery store couldn't have an on-line Web form with pictures so that you click out an order and then they deliver it.

Listings hosted on **www.internet-is.com:**

- CyberMedia Inc.
- Internet Information Systems
- Library Solutions Institute and Press
- Myers Equity Express
- Net Guru Technologies Inc.
- San Francisco Bay Area Parent Magazine
- The Skornia Law Firm

Listings hosted on **marketplace.com:**

- Harmony Games
- INFOMARK
- Information Law Alert
- Interactive Publishing Alert
- The Maloff Company
- MarketPlace.com, The Internet Information Mall
- Online Bookstore

The Online Bookstore (meaning no disparagement to the many fine independent booksellers around the world) has the advantage that IT HAS EVERYTHING in print, right there, right now.

Listings hosted on **www.visions.com:**

- Alpha Research Centre Incorporated
- Canada Net Pages
- Canada Net Real Estate
- Canada Wild Salmon Products
- Project Rainbow
- Sun-West Cellular Products Inc.
- Synapse 6000

Listings hosted on **www.kiosk.net:**

- Elvis Stamps
- Hyatt Regency Washington
- John Lennon and James Dean Postage Stamps
- Marilyn Monroe postage Stamps
- The National Library of Poetry
- Saudi Arabia, Ministry of Information

If you figure out what the Saudi government is doing in a stamp outlet, you tell me at chseiter@aol.com.

Listings hosted on **www.fractals.com:**

- The Fractal Images Company
- Gramma's Rose Garden Inn
- Linda Sy Skin Care

- Mason-McDuffie Real Estate
- The Musical Offering
- University Press Books/Berkeley

`fractals.com` is a Berkeley, CA server. I can personally vouch for Gramma's as the coziest B&B in the Peoples' Republic of Berkeley.

Listings hosted on **www.ip.net:**

- Electronics and Networking Services
- International Communication Corporation
- Internet Presence & Publishing
- Krema Nut Company
- New Media Associates
- THINK BIG! WorldStore

`ip.net` is devoted to designing Internet access for other businesses — give 'em a call.

Listings hosted on **www.sccsi.com:**

- The Advant Home
- Craig Stewart Studio
- Da Vinci Design Company
- South Coast Computing Services Inc.
- Webvertising
- Windsurfing Sports

Listings hosted on **www.clark.net:**

- AutoPages of Internet
- ClarkNet
- Criswell Chevrolet/Lotus of Maryland
- John Makulowich: Internet Training
- NetworX, Inc.
- Rolls Royce of Beverly Hills

Yes, I know — you've been wondering all along if you could order a Rolls Royce on the Web. Good news for you! There are very nice pictures of the cars, and remember — there's a new less-expensive model for 1995.

Listings hosted on **www.srv.net:**

- The Craft Boutique
- Healthy Alternatives
- Innovations
- Innovative Design, Inc.
- UltraVend
- The Yellowstone Outdoorsman

Triangle Virtual Reality (referring to the Research Triangle in North Carolina, where USENET, among other things, was invented) is a must-see stop on your Web tour.

Listings hosted on **www.trinet.com:**

- Allen Marketing Group
- Information Services for Agriculture, Inc.
- K Computing
- Triangle Virtual Reality (TRIVR)
- TSI Soccer

Listings hosted on **www.automatrix.com:**

- Automatrix
- Banner Graphics
- D.J. Panzl, Inc.
- KC Computing
- O'Donnell, Wicklund, Pigozzi & Peterson Architects, Inc.

Listings hosted on **www.demon.co.uk:**

- Demon Internet Ltd.
- The Internet Bookshop
- KarlBridge
- Pilkington Micro-Electronics
- Ross Anderson Consulting

The Internet bookshop on demon.co.uk is one way to buy *The Internet For Macs For Dummies Quick Reference* in the UK.

Listings hosted on **ftp.netcom.com:**

- Arent Fox Kintner Plotkin & Kahn
- Collectors Network
- Global Prepress Center

By the way, I expect an explosion of commercial servers on `netcom.com` soon, because they're one of the biggest dial-up Internet services.

Listings hosted on **www.utw.com:**

- Bonneville International Corporation
- Computer Recyclers
- Execusoft
- First Security Bank, Corporate Trust Department
- Utah Wired

Listings hosted on **netmedia.com:**

- Alternative Textbooks
- Association of Bay Area Governments
- Bay Area Restaurant Guide
- Internet Media Services
- Stanford Shopping Center

`netmedia.com` takes eclecticism to new heights. The Association of Bay Area Governments is an excuse for county supervisors to try out the restaurants in the Guide, and little else. Stanford Shopping Center in Palo Alto is where people who made serious money in Silicon Valley collect to unload it — it's a sort of Rodeo Drive North.

Listings hosted on **storefront.xor.com:**

- Capella Networking
- The Colorado Internet Cooperative Association
- The Internet StoreFront
- Softpro Books
- XOR Network Engineering

Listings hosted on **www.charm.net:**

- Charm Net
- CyberGroup, Inc.

- CyberWeb SoftWare
- Internet Business Connection
- North Carolina Quality Furniture

Here are more ways to connect. Check out Internet Business Connection to put your very own new cyberbusiness on the Web!

Listings hosted on **www.icw.com**:

- Access Market Square
- Due North Multimedia
- InterConnect West

Listings hosted on **www.service.com**:

- Auction Directory & News
- Palo Alto Weekly
- Science Television
- US West

Listings hosted on **www.interaccess.com**:

- Chicago Mercantile Exchange
- InterAccess
- NetBoy
- Virtual Design Center

Listings hosted in **sashimi.wwa.com**:

- Entrepreneurs on the Web
- Mighty Dog Designs
- The Mouse-Board
- Romance — Elegant Lingerie and Gifts

I probably shouldn't tell you this, but if you don't have anything better to do on a rainy Saturday afternoon, check the Web lingerie catalog on `sashimi.wwa.com`.

Listings hosted on **xmission.com**:

- A+ Marketing
- AOI Travel

- Delphi Internet Services
- Sell-it on the WWW

`xmission.com` not only offers a way to put yourself on the Web, but also offers a gateway to Delphi, one of the few real Internet services designed for the average person.

Listings hosted in **kaleidoscope.bga.com**:

- Blue Square
- The Global City
- Kaleidoscope Communications Inc.
- The Reference Press

Listings hosted on **nyweb.com**:

- New York Apple Tours
- New York Web
- The Online Ad Agency

Listings hosted on **gnn.com**:

- Global Network Navigator (GNN)
- Nolo Press' Self-Help Law Center
- O'Reilly & Associates, Inc.

All servers are not created equal. The innocent looking Navigator under `gnn.com` is a *must see* information resource for WWW business. It's near the end of these listings, but you may want to try it first.

Listings hosted on **www.netmarket.com**:

- 800-THE-ROSE
- The NetMarket Company
- Noteworthy Music Compact Discs

Listings hosted in **www.elpress.com**:

- Cellular One
- Electronic Press, Inc.
- Staunton, Virginia

Appendix E

Glossary

These are all terms you are likely to encounter while roaming the Net or planning your next adventure.

address

A person's Internet address is the line with the @, as in `chseiter@aol.com`. From the Internet's point of view, an address is a set of four numbers, such as 132.34.115.31. The numbers correspond to a name that you can remember, such as `zapp.com` or `simple.net`.

alt

The newsgroups with the highest entertainment value are all in the unofficial alternative newsgroup hierarchy, and their names start with `alt`.

Anarchie

Anarchie is a Macintosh shareware program that performs Archie searches. It's very good, and every national on-line service has it in Mac software libraries.

anonymous FTP

Anonymous FTP is a procedure for logging into computers that maintain file archives that are accessible to anyone. You use *anonymous* as your user name and your e-mail address as your password.

AppleTalk

Apple's own set of hardware and software for managing local area networks. It's a slow protocol, best for smaller networks.

Archie

Archie is the basic Internet system for finding files. An Archie server is a computer that has lists of available archived files all over the Internet.

archive

An archive is just a collection of files. At a site that maintains archives, someone is responsible for updating files and checking the archive for viruses.

ASCII

ASCII stands for *A*merican *S*tandard *C*ode for *I*nformation *I*nter-change, a definition that associates each character with a number from 0 to 255. An ASCII file is a text file of characters.

backbone

A high-speed set of network connections. On the Internet, this usually means the NSFNET, a government-funded set of links between large computer sites.

BBS

Shorthand for *bulletin board system*. A BBS can be an old Mac II in a garage or a gigantic system with 10,000 users. Get a copy of *Boardwatch* magazine.

binary file

A file of 0s and 1s, which can represent pictures and sound as well as text.

binhex

A file transmission fix-up. Most mail programs can only handle ASCII, so a binhex utility program converts binary programs to ASCII so that people can mail you a binary file. At the receiving end, you have to decode the file back to binary with the programs BinHex (4.0 or 5.0), HQXer, or uudecode.

BITNET

A large network that passes material back and forth to the Internet.

biz

A newsgroup where you find discussions that have to do with (gasp!) money. Generally, you're not supposed to use other newsgroups for commercial purposes.

bridge

A bridge is a set of hardware and software that lets two different networks appear to be a single larger network to people connecting from outside the system.

chat

If you send messages to an electronic mailbox, that's e-mail. If you're sending messages back and forth to someone in real time, that's chat. See *IRC*.

ClariNet

ClariNet is a special newsgroup system that provides first-rate commercially important news and charges a fee. Some Internet service providers carry it; some don't.

com

This is the top-level domain name that identifies businesses.

communication software

This is the software that controls your modem and dials out to other networks. Mac examples are ZTerm, Microphone, White Knight, and the communications modules of Microsoft Works and ClarisWorks.

comp

The term comp in the middle of a newsgroup name means that the discussions will be computer-oriented. I'm sorry to report that the majority of these groups are oriented towards Unix or PCs, not Macintoshes.

country code

A top-level domain name that identifies a site by country: well.sf.ca.us, for example, has the country code us because San Francisco is physically, if not emotionally, part of the United States.

CPT

The file extension .cpt at the end of a filename means the file was compressed with Compact Pro. You can expand it either with that program or with one of the StuffIt series from Aladdin Software.

DIALOG

A huge information service, managed by Lockheed, with lots of technical databases.

dial-up

A dial-up connection is one that works only while you're connected by phone. The other type of connection is direct, where you're wired to a network and are connected all the time.

domain

An Internet site address has two parts, the domain and the top-level domain name. For America Online — aol.com — aol is the domain name and com is the top-level part. The domain roughly corresponds to the name of a particular network.

DOS

The original operating system that Microsoft cooked up (actually, Microsoft bought it in a one-sided deal) for IBM PCs. Don't bother looking in DOS file collections.

edu

Usually, this is the Internet address identifier for a university. The universities of the United States are the reason the Internet is the vast wonderland it is today.

e-mail

Electronic mail. It's a message you compose on your computer to be received on someone else's computer, although some services let your message be delivered as a fax or (this sounds weird, but it's true) *an actual piece of paper!*

Ethernet

An Ethernet network is a very common, much faster alternative to Apple's original built-in networking stuff. Newer Macs for business now have Ethernet capability as part of the system.

Eudora

A Macintosh program for handling e-mail. The first versions were shareware, but now it's a commercial program from QualComm software.

FAQ

*F*requently *A*sked *Q*uestions. Trust me, your questions will be just like anyone else's. When you sign up with an Internet service provider — and before you make any contributions to newsgroups— read the FAQ files that are prominently displayed in menus. This saves you embarrassment and saves everyone else from your three-millionth-time newbie questions.

Fetch

A truly wonderful Macintosh FTP program from Dartmouth, available from all Internet service providers.

finger

On Unix-based Internet systems, finger is a utility that lets you get a profile of a user (including the user's real name).

flame

A flame is the sort of extreme opinion that the sender probably wouldn't have the nerve to deliver in person. Although some Internet old-timers seem to generate four flames a day, I think that as a matter of decorum you should never flame (it's a verb or a noun) anyone ever, no matter what.

freenet

There are about 30 or 40 freenets around the United States. These
are networks that don't charge you a monthly or per-hour fee.
Cool, huh? Your local librarian is likely to have the phone
numbers.

freeware

Freeware is software that is offered by its author for no charge.
This is different from shareware (see *shareware*). There's some
amazingly good freeware on the Net.

FTP

FTP stands for *file transfer protocol*. On the Internet, it usually
refers to a Unix-system utility program that lets you collect files
from archives at other sites.

FTP-by-mail

FTP-by-mail is a way to use e-mail to get files sent to you automatically from FTP sites, even if your own Internet service
provider doesn't have FTP implemented.

gateway

A gateway is hardware that lets messages be sent between two
different kinds of networks. You need a gateway, for example, to
communicate at network speeds between a Macintosh AppleTalk-
based network and a Unix-based network.

GIF

GIF stands for *graphics interchange format*—you see it as a file
extension on picture files as `flower.gif`. GIF files are very
common on the Internet, and most sites offer a shareware
program called GIFwatcher to read them. Adobe Photoshop and
other large image-handling programs can also work with GIF files.

gnu

Every time you look in a big archive, you see gnu folders. The
Free Software Foundation has developed gnu as a sort of Unix-
clone operating system, complete with C-language compiler and
lots of utilities, that it distributes for free, as a matter of principle.

Gopher

A Gopher is a file search-and-retrieval system that's usually the
right basic Internet tool for finding the file you want. For the
Macintosh, there's TurboGopher.

gov

Gov is the top-level name, or zone, for any type of governmental organization.

host

Most kinds of Internet access using a modem will have you dialing a host computer that's a big computer with its own Internet address.

HQX

When you see this as a file extension, it means that the file is in binhex (see *binhex*) format. You have to decode it to get the original file, and the easiest way to decode it is with HQXer.

HQXer

As you can guess from the name, this shareware utility processes files into and out of `.hqx` format. It's available in the libraries of every Internet service provider.

hypertext

Hypertext is a set of text files in which individual words link one file to the next.

HyTelnet

This program can be used to manage telnet functions, but it can also be used off-line as a comprehensive directory of telnet sites.

Internet protocol (IP)

A set of definitions that governs transmission of individual packets of information on the Internet.

Internet Society

A bunch of good people who discuss policies and make recommendations about Internet management.

InterNIC

The name stands for *Inte*rnet *N*etwork *I*nformation *C*enter. The word *InterNIC* turns up on the menus of many Internet service providers, and it's a good place to look for the history and future of the Net.

InterSLIP

A freeware program from Intercon that works with MacTCP to give your Mac a SLIP connection.

IRC

IRC stands for *I*nternet *R*elay *C*hat, an on-line forum of almost unimaginable liveliness that's offered by real Internet providers, such as Delphi.

jpeg

A compressed file format for images.

Jughead

Because there was a program called Archie and another called Veronica, someone decided that Jughead would be a good name for a Gopher searching tool.

Kermit

A slow but reliable file transfer protocol named, in fact, after the frog on *The Muppet Show*.

LISTSERV

LISTSERV programs manage mailing lists by sending messages automatically to everyone on a given list.

log in

Log in and log on are different terms for making contact with a remote computer. They're used interchangably.

Mac Binary

A special format for storing Macintosh binary files on other computers.

MacSLIP

An alternative to InterSLIP.

MacTCP

Apple's program (a Control Panel, actually) that you need to use a SLIP account. MacTCP translates your files and messages into Internet-compatible chunks of information.

MacWAIS

An excellent shareware program for WAIS, the *W*ide *A*rea *I*nformation *S*erver.

mail server

A mail server is a program on a host computer that saves your mail for you until you make a dial-up connection and have a chance to download your mail and read it.

Matrix

Lots of early Net visionaries use the term *Matrix* to denote the total of all connected computers in the world. It used to be used as a cool name for the Internet plus everything else.

mil

The top-level domain name of military sites on the Internet. Just about all U.S. military sites are Internet sites.

MIME

This acronym stands for *M*ultipurpose *I*nternet *M*ail *E*xtension, an Internet standard that lets you add sound and images to e-mail. It's not widely implemented yet, but it will be.

mirror

A mirror site is an archive that keeps a copy of the files in another site.

misc

Newsgroups that don't fit under any other recognizable category get put into `misc`.

modem

The device that lets your computer make telephone calls to other computers.

moderated

A moderated newsgroup has someone who filters out the really pointless or offensive material, leaving only moderately pointless or offensive messages.

Mosaic

Mosaic is the original freeware program for access to the World Wide Web hypertext system.

MUD

*M*ulti-*U*ser *D*ungeons are on-line fantasy games that can have dozens of players.

MUSE

*M*ulti-*U*ser *S*imulated *E*nvironments are a sort of highbrow MUD. A multiplayer version of the Mac game SimCity would be a MUSE.

NCSA

National Center for Supercomputing Applications, managed by the University of Illinois, is the home of Mosaic, along with lots of big computers.

network

Any set of computers that can communicate directly with each other constitutes a network.

newsgroup

A collection of people and messages on a particular topic of interest.

node

The term *node* in Internet context means a central computer that's part of an Internet-connected network. Sometimes used interchangeably with *site* or *host.*

NSFNET

The National Science Foundation *Net* is a principal Internet traffic carrier.

packet

A block of information, complete with addresses for destination and source, traveling over the Internet.

page

The basic unit of the World Wide Web information service is the page. Pages are linked by hypertext references to other pages.

password

OK, you know what a password is. Just try to think of a nonobvious password (usually, it shouldn't be a real word from a dictionary, much less your nickname) to save yourself potential grief.

PDIAL

The PDIAL list, available on every Internet service, is a regularly updated registry of public Internet access providers.

ping

An Internet program that is used to determine if a site is still active.

point of presence

A local phone number for high-speed access maintained by an Internet provider.

POP

*P*ost *O*ffice *P*rotocol is an e-mail protocol used for downloading mail from a mail server.

ppp

Point to Point Protocol is an alternative to SLIP for dial-up full Internet access. You would use MacPPP instead of InterSLIP or MacSLIP for this kind of connection. Your Internet service provider's system administrator will tell you which to use.

protocol

A protocol is a definition that controls communication on a network.

rec

Newsgroups for recreational purposes are signaled with `rec`. There's plenty of overlap between `rec` and `alt`, in practice.

RFC/RFD

*R*equests *F*or *C*omment and *R*equests *F*or *D*iscussion are study-group documents with an important role in settling general Internet questions about design and use.

rlogin

An alternative to telnet, rlogin is a Unix command for connecting to remote computers.

router

A router is a gateway (see *gateway*) between two networks that use Internet protocol.

sci

Serious research newsgroups in science and mathematics belong to this newsgroup hierarchy.

SEA

This file extension stands for *self-extracting archive*. If you double-click a `.sea` file, it usually turns itself into a folder containing an application and some documentation files.

server

A computer that stores files as a central resource for other computers, called clients, that can connect to the server to get files for themselves.

shareware

Shareware is software you can download free to test. If you like it and use it, you are obliged as a matter of honor to send the requested payment to the author.

SIT

Files compressed with StuffIt from Aladdin Software show this file extension. You can expand them with UnStuffIt, available from all the national on-line services and most bulletin boards.

SLIP

*S*erial *L*ine *I*nternet *P*rotocol lets you become a dial-up Internet site. You also need MacTCP to make a SLIP connection with a Macintosh. SLIP is an alternative to PPP.

SMTP

The *S*imple *M*ail *T*ransport *P*rotocol is the e-mail protocol standard for the Internet.

soc

The soc newsgroups on social issues overlap many of the alt social issue newsgroups.

TAR

This file extension indicates files compressed with a special Unix program. You can expand them with StuffIt Deluxe.

TCP/IP

The whole system, *T*ransport *C*ontrol *P*rotocol and *I*nternet *P*rotocol, makes up a standard guideline for network hardware and software design.

telnet

The core of all Internet services is the Unix utility telnet, a program that lets users connected to one host dial up a different Internet host.

terminal

In the old days, a terminal could only receive and send characters to the real computer at the other end of the wires. A terminal program lets your sophisticated Macintosh mimic this primitive arrangement.

thread

A series of connected messages in a newsgroup.

TurboGopher

A brilliant Macintosh Gopher program for searching all the files of the Internet. As freeware, TurboGopher is available everywhere in the libraries of on-line services.

Unix

The operating system that runs the Internet. Developed over many years, it's capable of meeting any networking challenge and is very thrifty with computing resources. The downside consequence of these virtues is that Unix is hard for beginners to use.

USENET

The network, linked at different points to the Internet, that supports all the newsgroups.

uu

Uuencode is a program that turns binary files into ASCII files so that you can send them through e-mail. Uudecode takes the files back to binary. Mac shareware utilities for this function are available in most libraries.

Veronica

Veronica is a program that searches for files over all available Gopher servers, making it the program to use whenever it's available. Higher-level searches are preferable to direct use of Archie.

vt 100/102

These are two very common terminals and, hence, two very common terminal-software options. As a first guess, pick `vt100` as the terminal setting when you dial up almost any service using standard communications software.

WAIS

Wide Area Information Servers are text databases with a superior search method that looks inside the text rather than just looking at document titles.

Windows

An attempt to stick a Macintosh-like face on the ugly reality of DOS.

WWW

World Wide Web is an Internet service consisting of hypertext-linked documents. When we all have faster Macs and faster connections, WWW will probably be the best kind of Internet facility because it's so easy for beginners to operate.

whois

A command available on some Internet services to find the real name of a user based on the user's screen name.

X, Y, and ZMODEM

XMODEM is a 15-year-old file transfer protocol; YMODEM is newer; and ZMODEM is the fastest and best.

z

Another type of Unix-system compressed file extension, also expandable with UnStuffIt.

ZIP

The most common compressed-file format for PCs. Unless it's a text file, you probably won't be able to do anything with a `.zip` file on a Mac even if you expand it, so don't bother unless there's a compelling reason to put yourself through the trouble.

Index

(continued)

IDG BOOKS WORLDWIDE REGISTRATION CARD

RETURN THIS
REGISTRATION CARD
FOR FREE CATALOG

Title of this book: **INTERNET FOR MACS FOR DUMMIES QR**

My overall rating of this book: ❏ Very good [1]   ❏ Good [2]   ❏ Satisfactory [3]   ❏ Fair [4]   ❏ Poor [5]

How I first heard about this book:

❏ Found in bookstore; name: [6]   ❏ Book review: [7]

❏ Advertisement: [8]   ❏ Catalog: [9]

❏ Word of mouth; heard about book from friend, co-worker, etc.: [10]   ❏ Other: [11]

What I liked most about this book:

What I would change, add, delete, etc., in future editions of this book:

Other comments:

Number of computer books I purchase in a year: ❏ 1 [12]   ❏ 2-5 [13]   ❏ 6-10 [14]   ❏ More than 10 [15]

I would characterize my computer skills as: ❏ Beginner [16]   ❏ Intermediate [17]   ❏ Advanced [18]
❏ Professional [19]

I use ❏ DOS [20]   ❏ Windows [21]   ❏ OS/2 [22]   ❏ Unix [23]   ❏ Macintosh [24]   ❏ Other: [25]_____
(please specify)

I would be interested in new books on the following subjects:
(please check all that apply, and use the spaces provided to identify specific software)

❏ Word processing: [26]   ❏ Spreadsheets: [27]

❏ Data bases: [28]   ❏ Desktop publishing: [29]

❏ File Utilities: [30]   ❏ Money management: [31]

❏ Networking: [32]   ❏ Programming languages: [33]

❏ Other: [34]

I use a PC at (please check all that apply): ❏ home [35]   ❏ work [36]   ❏ school [37]
❏ other: [38] _____

The disks I prefer to use are ❏ 5.25 [39]   ❏ 3.5 [40]   ❏ other: [41]_____

I have a CD ROM: ❏ yes [42]   ❏ no [43]

I plan to buy or upgrade computer hardware this year: ❏ yes [44]   ❏ no [45]

I plan to buy or upgrade computer software this year: ❏ yes [46]   ❏ no [47]

Name: _____ Business title: [48]

Type of Business: [49]

Address (❏ home [50]   ❏ work [51]/Company name: _____)

Street/Suite#

City [52]/State [53]/Zipcode [54]: _____ Country [55]

❏ **I liked this book!**
You may quote me by name in future IDG Books Worldwide promotional materials.

My daytime phone number is _____

IDG BOOKS

THE WORLD OF
COMPUTER
KNOWLEDGE

❏ YES!

Please keep me informed about IDG's World
of Computer Knowledge. Send me the latest
IDG Books catalog.

BUSINESS REPLY MAIL

FIRST CLASS MAIL   PERMIT NO. 2605   SAN MATEO, CALIFORNIA

IDG Books Worldwide
155 Bovet Rd
San Mateo CA 94402-9833